For more from Del Chatterson's Uncle Ralph:

DIYBusinessPlan.com
http://www.diybusinessplan.com/

Learn about Entrepreneurship
http://learningentrepreneurship.com

Ezine Articles on Business and Entrepreneurship
http://ezinearticles.com/?expert=Delvin_R._Chatterson

Uncle Ralphs' e2eForum Blog
http://e2eforum1.blogspot.ca

Business is Like Golf Blog:_
http://businessislikegolf.blogspot.com/

Or follow Del on:

LinkedIn: http://ca.linkedin.com/in/delchatterson

Twitter: http://twitter.com/Del_UncleRalph

Facebook: https://www.facebook.com/YourUncleRalph

And don't miss Uncle Ralph's new book for Entrepreneurs:

"Don't Do It the Hard Way"

**"A wise man learns from the mistakes of others;
only a fool insists on making his own".**

©2014

The Complete Do-It-Yourself Guide to Business Plans

"It's about the process, not the product"

New, Revised and Expanded, Second Edition

Your Uncle Ralph, **Delvin R. Chatterson**

authorHOUSE®

AuthorHouse™
1663 Liberty Drive
Bloomington, IN 47403
www.authorhouse.com
Phone: 1-800-839-8640

Throughout this Guide and in the Real life Stories, the actual individual names and business details have been changed to protect the subjects of each story. Any apparent use of real names is purely coincidental.

Published by AuthorHouse 03/10/2014

ISBN: 978-1-4918-6552-1 (sc)
ISBN: 978-1-4918-6551-4 (hc)
ISBN: 978-1-4918-6550-7 (e)

Library of Congress Control Number: 2014903238

Any people depicted in stock imagery provided by Thinkstock are models, and such images are being used for illustrative purposes only. Certain stock imagery © *Thinkstock.*

This book is printed on acid-free paper.

Dedicated to the principle that entrepreneurs who do better for themselves will also do better for their families, employees, customers and suppliers; their communities and the planet.

Do better.

ACKNOWLEDGEMENTS

This Guide is made more valuable, interesting and useful, thanks to the input of all the clients, consultants, bankers, business partners, investors and associates that I have worked with during the last thirty years and more. I could not possibly name them all. Some may recognize themselves in the real life stories and examples that I have used in the Guide and I apologize if they remember it differently or I neglected to mention all the lessons we learned together.

I appreciate and respect all the business planning guides, textbooks and online resources that I have referred to in developing my own approach and advice. I recommend many of these resources to the reader as useful complementary input to their business planning and management processes.

The feedback and suggestions from readers, friends and associates on the First Edition have contributed immensely to making this Second Edition a better Guide to Business Plans. I appreciate also that the quality of this publication has been greatly enhanced by the active support and professional services offered by my publisher AuthorHouse and Author Solutions LLC.

And most importantly, thank you to my talented and patient wife, Penny Rankin, who supported, encouraged, challenged, edited and improved every revision.

Thank you.

CAN I HELP YOU
WITH YOUR BUSINESS PLAN?

Well, this is what clients and bankers have said about the Business Plans that I've worked on with them:

- *Very well done! This answers all our questions and I can get approval quickly for you."* Lending officer, CIBC.

- *"This is exactly what we like to see in a Business Plan."* Account Manager, Business Development Bank of Canada.

- *"Now we have a documented strategy and financial projections that help us understand the business potential and take it to the next level."* Partners in a telemarketing service business.

- *"Finally we have a plan we can work with. Thanks Del, we never would have made it without you."* Two experienced executives launching a freight brokerage business.

- *"I would not hesitate to recommend Del ... to anyone seeking professional guidance in making their business grow."* Owner, Retail Business.

- *"Del respects and understands the entrepreneur... he led us to focus on the most important issues."* Entrepreneur, Office Furniture.

- *"His experience and expertise were utilized to develop a bullet proof business plan... the plan will certainly attract new investors."* President, Procurement Services Business.

- *"Hey Del, they liked the Plan and we're getting the loans!"* Entrepreneurs purchasing a garage/car wash business.

I expect to hear the same happy feedback from you after you read the Complete Do-It-Yourself Guide and apply it to your own Business Plans.

It will make a difference:
An easier process and better results.

CONTENTS

INTRODUCTION TO THE GUIDE

"It's about the process, not the product"

My objective with this Second edition of *The Complete Do-It-Yourself Guide to Business Plans* is to provide an expanded and enhanced version of the Guide, based on readers' feedback from the First Edition published in 2010.

This edition includes new material, real-life case studies, sample Business Plans and more information, tools, tactics, and techniques to help you prepare a better Business Plan.

Preparing a Business Plan remains an important and necessary requirement for every business; but for most business owners it is not an easy task.

Even with this Guide you may need the assistance of others – your banker, accountant, consultant or associates. But the Guide will help you to get the most out of the process and prepare a Business Plan that gets the results that you want – for a business start-up, new financing, growth and profitability, even sale and exit from the business, if you are at that stage.

Every entrepreneur needs to prepare and use an effective, documented business plan to provide direction to the management team and help them deliver the desired results.

But most importantly, I want to emphasize throughout that *the primary value in preparing a solid business plan comes from the process, not the product.*

The product is a valuable and necessary document, but the real value to the entrepreneur will be in the process of assessing the marketing opportunities, developing business strategies, testing marketing and operating plans, and evaluating the expected financial results under alternative scenarios.

This process (if well done, according to the methods that I will describe in this Guide) will lead you to prepare a plan for the business that is realistic, achievable, well understood and supported by all of the stakeholders involved – owners, managers, staff, lenders and investors.

My intent is to provide everything you need to "do-it-yourself" and prepare your own Business Plan, but you will also learn how to direct other participants in the process – your staff and your consultants or advisors.

I will cover all the aspects of completing a successful business plan. You will know that your plan is successful when it helps you get the financing you need and it leads you to building and growing a profitable business.

We will discuss the purpose of doing a business plan; choices of different business concepts, financial structures and strategies; business plan content, style and layout; and how to prepare a complete set of financial projections.

The Complete Do-It-Yourself Guide to Business Plans is a consolidation of everything that I have learned from the preparation or analysis of dozens of business plans as an entrepreneur, executive, and consultant. It incorporates the best practices that I have found over the past thirty years to achieve the desired results for business owners.

In addition to this guide you should take advantage of the other tools and guides available from Uncle Ralph at the website http://www.diybusinessplan.com and sign-up for the additional material that will help you advance your plans.

You will also find useful ideas, information and inspiration for entrepreneurs at the **e2eforum Blog** of Uncle Ralph at http://e2eforum1.blogspot.com or the **Business is like Golf Blog** at: http://businessislikegolf.blogspot.com.

With all these ideas, tools and information, I am confident that you will get great value out of the process, as well as prepare a dynamite business plan that gets you the results you want.

INTRODUCTION TO UNCLE RALPH

Del Chatterson is your Uncle Ralph

Before you spend your time and money on this Second edition of **The Complete Do-It-Yourself Guide to Business Plans** you have a right to know, "Who is Uncle Ralph and how can he help me prepare a Business Plan that gets the results I want?"

So here is my story.

I am your *"Uncle Ralph"*. You can call me Del.

I am a business consultant, executive, entrepreneur, writer, runner, golfer and photographer. I also play hockey and guitar. I am recently re-married; have two adult kids and two grandsons. I am a small town boy from the Rocky Mountains of British Columbia in Western Canada, now living in the fascinating, multicultural, bilingual, French Canadian city of Montreal, Quebec.

My background is Engineer from UBC in Vancouver and MBA from McGill in Montreal. I have extensive experience in the corporate world, management consulting and as an entrepreneur with my own businesses. My corporate experience included financial analysis and systems integration projects, purchasing and materials management. In management consulting, I was six years with Coopers and Lybrand working with businesses across Canada and in Europe and Central America. I have also worked as a business consultant with many entrepreneur clients in partnership with the Business Development Bank of Canada (BDC).

As an entrepreneur, I was eight years growing a distribution business, TTX Computer Products, from zero to $20 million per year; then two years to take it into and out of an unsuccessful merger; followed by management of my own business consulting firm, DirectTech Solutions, working with Internet start-ups and other owner-managed businesses. I have assisted entrepreneurs in a wide variety of industries at different stages of the business life cycle facing challenges that ranged from cash flow issues, to strategic direction to performance improvement and exit strategies.

Your Uncle Ralph comes from all that experience plus everything that I have learned from the good and bad managers that I have worked with over the years. Coincidentally, Ralph is my secret middle name and was my father's first name. Uncle Ralph is definitely much wiser than I am and has experienced more than I could possibly have lived through myself.

Uncle Ralph's interest is to share his ideas, experience and advice with other executives, entrepreneurs and managers to help improve their businesses and their lives. Of course I will also learn something in the process and look forward to sharing that too.

My own first Business Plan was a few ideas scratched out on paper with a rough budget that showed how we might actually be able to make money in a regional distribution business for computer hardware (TTX Computer Products). Nobody cared about it at that stage, except me and my partner. (But that's usually the first and best reason to prepare a Business Plan – to help the owners direct their decision making and action plans.)

We each put in a few thousand dollars and launched the business in April of 1986 with two employees. First month we did $10,000 in sales; not a bad start. (Even if I did keep the books open for an extra few days, just to meet our target.) We were profitable from the third month. And we kept profitable and growing that business up to $20 million in annual sales in eight years.

Of course, with growth we needed financing. To get it, the bank said, "OK, but we need two things - personal guarantees and a Business Plan." So we signed the personal guarantees and then I updated and documented our Business Plan and the spreadsheets. They were good enough to get us the first $50,000. The loans grew with the business until, with the merger, we were up to $4.8 million in bank lines of credit with <u>no personal guarantees</u>.

That's what a well-documented Business Plan can do for you! (A good track record of profitable growth also helps.)

My next start-up venture was an e-commerce business with a technology partner. Here we prepared more elaborate Business Plans to support the "dot-com" business model of high start-up and development costs, zero revenue and millions required in venture capital funding. We got great response to our Business Plan, negotiated deals with important strategic partners (another key use for your Business Plan) and started growing the business. When the dot-com bubble burst, we learned a lot more about business planning and managing sources of financing on the downside. We also learned when it was time to give up and come up with a new plan.

Over the last several years in my consulting business, I have worked with many different entrepreneurs and their investors to develop, evaluate, prepare and present Business Plans that delivered results.

I have also given courses in Business Planning at Concordia University in Montreal to help new entrepreneurs get their businesses started.

In recent years, I have gained international business exposure working as a Volunteer Advisor with CESO (Canadian Executive Services Overseas), an agency providing aid to countries in developing economies. It has been an enlightening experience to share my ideas and solutions with entrepreneurs who are facing the additional obstacles of high poverty, untrained workers and limited or ineffective infrastructure.

All this history and experience has been incorporated into writing this comprehensive *Complete Do-It-Yourself Guide to Business Plans*.

Please make good use of it for your own business.

Good luck and happy planning,

Your Uncle Ralph
Del Chatterson

March 2014

1

WHAT IS A BUSINESS PLAN?

Let's start by describing what we will deliver as a "Business Plan".

In simple terms, a business plan is a document that describes a business idea; the strategies and plans to turn that idea into a profitable business; and the financial results that are expected.

In more general terms, the business plan is a communications tool that will identify and confirm a business opportunity, define the proposed concept and approach to respond to that opportunity and support the strategies, operating plans and financial projections with solid logic and analysis.

It is not exactly a sales document, but it will be used to attract financing and convince strategic partners to participate in your plan.

An acceptable Business Plan will include a detailed and comprehensive description of the planned project or new venture with extensive relevant financial analysis and projections, plus supporting material that might include executive profiles, product brochures, facilities plans and market research studies.

The three key components in a Business Plan therefore, are:

1. A clear, persuasive description of the business opportunity and the strategies and action plans to respond to it;
2. A complete, detailed set of financial projections confirming the investment required and the expected future profitability; and

3. Appendices with additional objective reference material that supports all the assumptions and forecasts shown in the plan.

This Guide will explain how to prepare all the elements of a complete business plan package, how to get the most out of the process, and how to get the results you want from your plan.

2

Why Do You Need a Business Plan?

"It's the process, not the product."

Keep that phrase in mind as a reminder that the **value** of doing a Business Plan lies in the ***planning process***, not in the final product, which is simply an elaborate document. A useful and important document, of course, but less valuable than the analysis, decisions and strategic plans that come out of the process.

Every business needs one.
It's not just for start-ups or new product launches.

Documenting a Business Plan is an extremely useful process to focus the owners and the management team on their business model, strategies, and operating plans. The process will force consensus and decision making that might otherwise be neglected. It requires issues to be resolved and documented after testing alternative solutions and their financial consequences.

A well-documented business plan will help you communicate the most important elements of your strategy and plans to the people who need to know them most. Including you.

Maybe you've been successful in business for many years and never had a business plan. It's still a good idea for all the same reasons. And now is a good time.

Maybe you're ready to exit your business. Even better. A solid business plan will be the most important document you have to support the value of your business.

The most *common* reason for preparing a business plan, from my experience, is "*because the bank asked for one*."

That is probably why most readers of this Guide are here. And that is obviously a legitimate reason for doing one. (We'll discuss later why the bank is asking for one and what they want to see in it.)

The greatest value of a business plan, however, is always in the process – involving your management team in a thorough examination of your business; its purpose, its strategies and its plans to ensure success. When completed, all the key players will be more knowledgeable of the issues, the opportunities, the risks and the alternative paths considered; before committing to the final plan.

For a small business start-up, that management team may only be you. It's still a valuable exercise. It forces you to answer all the questions that you should ask yourself and that will certainly be asked by the next people to get involved.

With a well documented business plan you will be prepared.

Real Life Story: "Don't take that to the bank"

It started with "Hi Del, we found you on the Internet". A week later, I was sitting down with Peter, Paul and Mary to work with them on their start-up business plan.

Peter and Paul were two experienced executives in the computer hardware service business and Mary was Paul's wife. They wanted to quit their current jobs and start their own computer services business that would succeed where their current employers were failing. They had the necessary knowledge, experience and contacts to quickly get up to speed and win business from competitors.

But there were two major flaws in their initial plan. First, they had an unnamed additional partner who was currently the Purchasing Agent with a customer of their current employer and who was promising to switch a large contract from their employer to their new business. Oops!

Probably a firing offense as a conflict of interest for the partner and a breach of employment or non-compete agreements for Peter and Paul. We agreed to leave the third partner out of the deal, at least until he also had left his current job.

The second major flaw was their plan to attract both suppliers and customers with very generous payment terms. The exact opposite of the often recommended cash management policy of *"collect fast and pay slow"*, they intended to let their customers pay slow and have their suppliers paid fast. Certainly attractive for customers and suppliers, but a disaster for financing and profitability.

Not something to take to the bank to demonstrate good management capabilities and a plan to succeed. So we reverted to normal industry payment terms in the plan and focused on leveraging their strengths of market knowledge and technical expertise to attract customers and suppliers. That not only made the plan more presentable, but also reduced the start-up financing requirement from over $100,000 to less than $40,000.

These were valuable changes to their business plan resulting from the *process* of testing strategies and plans to see the real impact on operations and financial results.

They did succeed in getting financed and two years later were growing fast.

(Note: In all these Real life Stories, the actual names and business details have been changed to protect the innocent subjects involved in each story. Their stories are told here only for the purpose of helping other entrepreneurs get better results from their Business Plans.)

3

WHAT IS THE PROCESS?

Continuous recycling: rethinking, reviewing and rewriting.

Recently, while revising my lecture material for another course on business planning at Concordia University in Montreal, I spent some time reviewing other resources available from a wide variety of sources.

It was all very ***uninspiring***: Unconvincing in the reasons for doing a good business plan and entirely discouraging in describing the elaborate process for preparing one. Not likely to persuade busy, results-oriented, document-challenged entrepreneurs that it's a good idea and that they can do it for themselves.

My mission became clearer.

And I started to describe my own approach as ***"Recycling your Business Plan".*** That best describes the process I recommend: Start with a very simple document, then continuously review, revise and expand the plan to deal with more issues and answer more questions.

In that approach I'm reminded of the *"million dollar napkin"* that one entrepreneur boasts he used to start his business simply by responding to the challenge to put it all on a restaurant napkin.

And there are the thousands of successful businesses that were launched *"on the back of an envelope"*. It's a good way to start your business plan – **describe it in a few words on one page.**

Here are the steps that I recommend to "recycle" your business plan.

Each step is a version of your Business Plan that becomes more solid and detailed at each "recycling":

1. Describe the market opportunity, your concept, business strategy, company name and marketing slogan and reasons it will succeed – on one page (or napkin, or envelope).

2. Confirm that your personal objectives are consistent with your business objectives and that you have the skills, personality, experience, contacts and knowledge required (or explain how you will acquire them).

3. Collect and analyse data on your market, customers and competitors that confirm both the business opportunity and your ability to meet customer needs against competitive alternatives.

4. Do a business feasibility test at your estimated sales volumes, pricing and operating costs to determine profitability. Calculate the break-even sales level and compare it to your forecast sales.

5. Document in more detail your business concept and strategy and all the operating plans for facilities, organisation, operations, marketing and sales. Add a section on the risks considered and your planned response to anything that may not go according to plan.

6. Expand the financial analysis to include start-up costs, working capital required and the cash flow consequences to determine the financing required. How much, required when, and how will it be recovered? Test alternative scenarios to ensure that potential variations in sales forecasts and cost estimates still lead to profitability and that financing will be adequate.

7. Complete the business plan document and a full set of financial projections against a checklist of the requirements for your intended audience - management team, lenders, investors, or strategic partners. Add relevant supporting appendices.

8. Then recycle the essential elements to capture your Business Plan in a two-to-three page Executive Summary, in a 1-minute elevator pitch, and in a 10-20 slide PowerPoint presentation for alternate forms of brief introduction to your plan.

9. The final recycling step for your Business Plan is to continuously refer to it against your future operating results. After review, check whether the plan and objectives are still valid and then revise either your plans or your performance to achieve the objectives.

That's it.

These few simple steps will take you from a good idea to a well developed and fully documented Business Plan that will serve as a guide to management and will persuade others to invest in your plan.

Remember the objective is to arrive at that communications document that confirms the business opportunity, describes your strategy and operating plans, and presents the supporting research and financial projections to prove that it will be a profitable and successful business.

Recycling is good.

The following sections describe each of these steps in more detail.

4

CHECK YOUR PERSONAL OBJECTIVES

Are you sure you want to be your own boss?
Do you have what it takes?

Before you make the leap into starting your own business, ask yourself these four questions:

- Is it really a good personal career choice?
- What do I need to know to decide?
- How can I prepare myself?
- How do I get started?

In this section, I will help you find the answers to those key questions.

Who will succeed and who will not? Why and why not?

I often make the analogy that starting your own business is a lot like sky-diving – it seems like an exciting idea, but you're not likely to do it until you're pushed out the door. So what's pushing you?

In my case, I had literally been pushed out the door of a company that was winding down and my number finally came up. (Not a surprise, since I had spent the previous nine months closing facilities and letting people go; but a painful experience nonetheless.) Two other corporate job offers were soon presented to me, but I decided that it was time to take care of my own career plan and not let someone else decide what I was doing next. (Sound familiar?)

Besides, with an MBA and lots of experience, I was ready to prove that I was at least as good a manager and businessman as the "idiots" I had been working for. That might sound a little arrogant or angry, but it did keep me motivated through the early setbacks.

How about you? Do you really want to own your own business? Be your own boss?

The advantages are attractive, but don't forget the disadvantages that are an inevitable part of the choice.

Advantages

- Unlimited opportunity
- Freedom, independence
- Continuous challenge, variety
- Your choice of management style
- Responsible for and involved in, the whole business
- If the business does well, you do well

Disadvantages

- There are still limits to what you can do or control
- New pressures of more people now dependent on you
- Requires skills and knowledge you do not have
- Cannot leave it at the office
- Higher risk and less secure financial future
- If the business fails, it's now tougher to find a "real" job

To keep it all in perspective, here are some comments by other entrepreneurs that will help you think about what it means to be your own boss:

- "I used to work for someone that I called boss. Now I work for thirty people who call me boss."
- "I wanted to be my own boss. But now I have many bosses – my customers, my employees, my suppliers, the bank, the landlord, the government and the city! It's hard to satisfy them all."
- "It's still better than working for somebody else."
- "I'm the best boss I ever had!"

Which will apply to you and your business? Is that what you want?

Are you likely to succeed?

The next step is to assess whether you are the *"entrepreneurial type"*. It may be true that anyone can be an entrepreneur, but there are certain personal characteristics, preferences, attitudes and abilities that are essential to success.

You need to honestly assess each of these factors if you want to improve your chances to succeed as an entrepreneur:

- Personal expectations and preferences for variety and challenge in your life style, work environment; needs for recognition and compensation. Are they corporate or entrepreneurial?
- Personal strengths and weaknesses, will they help, or hurt, the business?
- Are your education, training, and contact network directly relevant to your business venture?
- Do you have the characteristics of successful entrepreneurs:
    - o Independent, confident, persistent, action-oriented, risk taking personality.
    - o Passionate, leader, achiever, communicator.

- Your foundation – family, physical, and financial. Are they solid or a distraction?
- Strategic relationships already in place – partners, suppliers, key customers, employees?
- Timing – now, or never? Too soon, too late?

Is entrepreneurship the right career choice for you?

The questions and approaches described above should help you decide and then to develop a plan to succeed with your chosen business venture.

Real Life Story: *"Don't quit your day job, yet."*

Many young daydreamers, and older ones that should know better, see entrepreneurship as their escape from a day job that is not meeting their needs.

"Surely, running my own business would be better than this!" Well, maybe not. The same reasons that you are not succeeding on the job may also be big obstacles to your success in business. And entrepreneurship will test skills and capacities that you have not tested before.

Consider the old IBM sales executive that retired early and ... bought a hot dog franchise. He probably used none of his skills and experience from IBM and then also discovered he did not have the patience or aptitude to manage low-budget customers and low-skill employees. Neither a good investment nor a good career decision.

Or consider the frustrated young computer technician that wanted to sell his skills directly to all those home office users that needed his expertise, instead of working so hard for a demanding network services manager and having to run around big corporate offices where nobody appreciated him. We chatted and he wanted to pay me to write a business plan that would get him started with a bank loan so that he could pay himself until he found some customers and signed some contracts.

Sounds simple, right? But no bank would ever finance that plan.

I had to persuade him to stop daydreaming; keep his money and keep his day job.

A better plan was to upgrade his technical skills and get some experience in management and sales with his current employer, so that he could then launch his own business in the same attractive corporate services environment. Too many unhappy computer technicians are already under-employed and under-paid in the difficult home office market.

Look before you leap.

5

FIND THE RIGHT BUSINESS OPPORTUNITY

Start with your personal knowledge, experience and contacts.

If you are satisfied that you have what it takes to succeed as an entrepreneur and you are still determined to proceed, then you need to consider which business opportunity best meets your entrepreneurial ambitions.

Here are some of the alternative business models to consider:

- Home based business, self-employed
- Multi-level marketing business
- Independent contractor – trade or professional
- Sales agent – insurance, real estate, financial services
- Franchise – retail, fast food, business services
- Independent business – local, national, global
- Retailer, hospitality or food services, consumer services
- Manufacturer, distributor, business services
- Internet or technology based business, online only
- Entrepreneurial role within a corporate environment

Your choices may be limited by your start-up resources; or may be obvious for the type of business that you want to be in. It may be appropriate to start with one type of business and evolve to another as your business grows – from a home office to an incorporated business or from a local retailer to a national franchisor.

Once those choices are considered and decisions are made, the next question is: What is my best business opportunity?

No point in day-dreaming at this point about how you would like to be rich and famous. **Be realistic** about your skills, talents, education and experience for the industry that you choose. You would not be the first high-powered corporate executive that failed at running a restaurant franchise.

Is your past success transferrable? Build on what you already know you can do and add what's missing with good strategic partnerships, managers, employees, advisors, or suppliers.

Your selection of a potential business opportunity should start with your **personal knowledge, experience, and contacts;** then be confirmed by doing your homework.

Yes, your "gut feel" and intuition are important too, but let's balance your feelings with the facts.

These are the initial questions to be answered:

- Which opportunities match my capabilities?
- What is the specific market need, current supplier deficiency, or problem that I can solve?
- What current solutions are available?
- What other options does the customer have?
- What is my proposed solution?
- Has the appeal of my solution been confirmed by market testing and customer feedback?
- Can I deliver the solution and make it profitable?

Market Research

A very important part of the homework required before you start your plan is the essential market research to confirm the market opportunity and identify the target markets and prospects, the current competition and potential customers buying behavior.

Market research should give you important quantitative and qualitative data on each of the following:

- The target market – most attractive segments, customers and opportunities.
- Growth potential – a growing market offers more opportunities for new businesses than a mature, well-developed market. Example: Mobile devices versus desktop computers.
- Customer characteristics, buying patterns – how will they find you and be persuaded to choose your solution to their problem?
- Current and future competition – what are the choices now and how will you be different?
- Test market – how do prospective customers respond to your pitch, price, and packaging?

The most convincing market feedback, of course, is a history of sales success.

If you do not yet have that, then maybe you can get letters of intent, conditional orders or at least enthusiastic endorsements from prospective customers.

Once you have collected all that solid market feedback you can more confidently define your concept and your business strategy to approach the market. The next step is to test financial feasibility.

6

TEST FINANCIAL FEASIBILITY

Can we make money at this?

Some initial feasibility tests will help you refine and develop your plan so that it leads you to build a growing and profitable business.

You will need to use the data you have collected from the market research, make some initial assumptions and then test alternative scenarios to determine how to make your business profitable.

Net Profit at breakeven is zero.

Above the breakeven level of sales your business becomes profitable. Below breakeven you are losing money.

Start with this list of data required to determine breakeven sales levels and compare them to your forecasts. Then the following steps and examples below will guide you through the process.

1. Forecast Unit Sales per month that you expect after the first year.
2. Determine average price and average cost per unit (if you have a mix of products or services, use the forecast total monthly sales revenue and the corresponding monthly cost of sales).
3. Calculate Average Gross Profit Margin, in three ways:

    a. $ Gross Margin per unit of sale = $ Price/unit – $ Cost/unit

    b. % Gross Margin per unit =$ Gross Margin per unit ÷ $ Price per unit, and

    c.   % Average Gross Margin = $ Gross Margin per month ÷ $ Sales per month

4. Estimate Fixed Expense per month including Administration, Overhead, Marketing and Sales expense, but not including those items already in the variable cost of sales above.

Now you have everything you need to calculate the breakeven level of sales and test whether your expected forecast sales revenue will be profitable.

Remember "breakeven" is that level of sales that will deliver just enough gross profit margin to cover the fixed expenses.

You can calculate your breakeven sales using these formulas:

- Breakeven $ Sales revenue = Fixed Expense ÷ %Gross Margin
- Breakeven Unit Sales = Fixed Expense ÷ $Gross Margin per unit

For example:

- Average selling price is $12.00 for each product sold; the average cost is $9.00
- Therefore, Average Gross Profit Margin = $3.00 per unit or 25% ($3 ÷ $12 = 25%).
- Monthly fixed operating cost is $24,000/mo. (Including salaries, rent, utilities, insurance, interest, marketing, etc. – everything payable monthly regardless of the level of sales.)
- Calculated <u>Breakeven Unit Sales</u>:
  = $24,000/month ÷ $3 per unit = 8000 units/month
  (i.e. @$12 each, sales of $96,000), or
- Calculated <u>Breakeven $ Sales Revenue</u>:
  = $24,000/month ÷ 25% = $96,000 sales
  (Confirming the unit sales calculation.)
- Breakeven profit of zero at $96,000/month:
  = ($96,000 Sales x 25% Gross Margin) – ($24,000/month Fixed Costs)

= $24,000 profit margin - $24,000 costs = $0 profit (as expected).

The conclusion, therefore, is that the business will only be profitable above sales of $96,000 per month, given the 25% profit margin and $24,000/month in fixed costs.

Two additional considerations should be included in your feasibility tests:

- **Recovery of start-up costs**
- **Cash flow breakeven**

Start-Up Costs:

Assume the investment cost to start this business is $180,000, which you want to amortize (pay back) over five years (60 months).

This requirement adds $3000 per month in depreciation allowance (i.e. $180,000 ÷ 60 months). That additional amount should be considered to determine what level of sales will provide for recovery of the total costs – the initial investment plus the monthly operating costs. In this example:

<u>Total Cost Recovery Breakeven:</u>

- Monthly Total Operating cost: $24,000 plus the $3000 in amortization of investment costs.
- Breakeven = ($24,000 + $3000) ÷ $3 = 9000 units. ($108,000 per month at $12 each)
- Alternatively, using % Gross Margin, Breakeven = ($24,000 + $3000) ÷ 25%GM = $108,000/mo. (same as above)

Financing Costs:

Borrowing to finance the investment of $180,000 may require loan capital payments of $6000 per month, which is higher than your depreciation allowance and is in addition to the monthly interest charges already included in the fixed operating costs.

This will affect your cash flow breakeven which is also important to ensure that your financing plan is adequate.

Total Cash Flow Breakeven:

- Monthly Cash operating cost: $24,000 including interest payments, plus the $6000 capital payments.
- Breakeven = ($24,000 + $6000) ÷ $3 per unit = 10,000 units. ($120,000 Sales)

These breakeven calculations provide appropriate benchmarks for you to assess the feasibility of your business under the initial assumptions for costs and revenues.

Now compare these breakeven sales levels to your sales forecasts to determine profitability:

FORECAST SALES > BREAKEVEN = PROFIT$$$!

If your forecasts do <u>not </u>lead to profitability, then you need to revise (or abandon) the plan. Do not simply increase your forecasts, unless you can support them with new data or different business conditions.

If new sales forecasts are not appropriate then perhaps the assumed costs can be improved. Either reducing product cost to increase Gross Profit margins or lowering the fixed monthly operating expenses will both reduce the level of sales for breakeven and improve the profitability at your forecast level of sales.

Once you have completed the feasibility tests and arrived at reasonable assumptions that deliver profitability, you are ready to get started on documenting your detailed business plan. You have confirmed the market opportunity, your personal capabilities and the approach that will turn it into a profitable business. The first recycling of your plan is done.

The next step is to make some strategic decisions, then develop your operating plans and financial projections in more detail.

7

GETTING STARTED

What business concept and structure will be the most likely to succeed?

Some initial decisions need to be made on the right business model and legal structure before starting to document your plan. Which will be best for your business?

At this point you should already have the initial ideas on paper for your defined market opportunity, your concept and approach to the market, business model and growth strategy.

These are the next decisions to be made:

- Legal structure
    - o Sole proprietorship, partnership, or corporation?
- Start-up process
    - o Build from zero?
    - o Buy an existing business?
    - o Rent a business (i.e. "buy" a franchise), or
    - o Assume leadership of a family business.

Your decision among these choices (to buy, build, rent or inherit) will depend on the actual realistic options available to you, your personal preferences, and the business concept or strategy that you plan to pursue.

Here are some of the issues to consider in making the right decision and getting started.

Legal Structure

A sole proprietorship may be the best choice for a self-employed entrepreneur in a trade or profession where the business is essentially providing an alternative source of personal income. If you are "working for yourself" no formal legal structure is required; revenue and expense are simply included on your personal tax return under "Business Income". It is a simple and low cost structure to start, or discontinue if necessary. Formal financial statements are still required, but you can probably prepare them yourself and you may not require an accountant to prepare your tax returns.

The disadvantages are that you have less flexibility in splitting business and personal income, both the timing and the amounts, and <u>you remain personally responsible for any business liabilities</u>.

This may be the biggest risk – that you are not protected from the liabilities that you incur through the business. They will be yours personally and your personal assets may be at risk unless you purchase liability insurance or you have limited liability agreements with everyone that you do business with. Both of those may be a good idea anyway; if they are practical and affordable.

In addition, a sole proprietorship is less attractive to potential employees, suppliers, lenders or investors for them to do business with. It is seen as having limited potential and perhaps less commitment from the owner. So you are pretty much on your own to finance and operate the business.

A business partnership may be the right structure if you want to share management responsibilities and add skills, knowledge and experience beyond your own. In a partnership of any kind, care should be taken to have clear, documented legal agreements that define your shared responsibilities and your shared participation in profits, assets and liabilities.

In some regulated professions or industries, you may not be allowed to incorporate and only a personally registered business or partnership is acceptable. Check with the regulatory authorities and your legal advisors to be sure that you are meeting the industry requirements.

For most businesses, I recommend **incorporation.**

An incorporated business is a strong indication to all observers of your commitment to a serious long-term business and makes the very important legal distinction between the business and its owner/shareholders.

The corporation is a separate legal entity that has rights, obligations and liabilities that are separate from those of the shareholders, whose liability is limited to their investment in the business.

The corporation is taxed separately, and differently, from its shareholder owners. Ownership and management are legally separated so that ownership can be sold or transferred without necessarily affecting the management team or operation of the business.

An incorporated business has the following additional advantages over other forms of legal structure:

- Clear separation of owner and management roles and responsibilities
- More attractive to other participants, such as lenders, investors, employees, customers and strategic partners
- Easy transfer or sale of ownership
- An indefinite life span, separate from the founders and owners
- Unlimited potential to grow and to be financed by additional shareholders, including the public.

There are, however, some disadvantages and additional costs associated with incorporation that must be recognized.

Incorporation is more expensive and complex than the other legal business structures to set up and will also create future obligations for annual reporting. You may require professional services from lawyers and accountants to meet all these obligations. Their fees will increase with the size and complexity of the business, from less than $1000 to several tens of thousands per year.

The incorporated business will also be required to pay corporate income taxes in addition to any taxes on income to the shareholders, effectively increasing the total tax paid by the business owners on their personal and business income. Rates and regulations will depend on the jurisdiction where your business operates.

All these additional costs and complexities need to be weighed against the potential advantages of operating an incorporated business compared to the alternatives of sole proprietorship or partnership.

Start-up Choices

Most business plans start from zero and build an idea into a profitable growing business. This Guide is primarily designed for those businesses that are initial start-ups, but it can be used for business planning at any stage of the business life cycle.

For start-ups and new entrepreneurs, the important alternatives to consider for getting into a business are: **build, buy, rent, or inherit.**

It may be difficult to arrange to inherit a business if you are not already in the family, but you can buy an existing business or "rent" one by buying a franchised business. Either of those options may reduce the unknowns and the risks associated with a start-up, but there are other important considerations.

Buying a Business

The advantages of buying an existing business are obvious:

- An existing entity with markets, customers, employees, suppliers, and facilities that can be evaluated
- Established operations and business relationships
- The company, its products and brands already known in the market
- Added value of working assets, plus the intangibles of "goodwill"
- Easier to assess opportunities for improvements and sales growth

Buying a business, however, also requires careful consideration of some new risks:

- Reliability of financial statements
- Unreported income or expenses from "cash" deals
- Mixing the owner's personal with business expenses
- Dependence on very few customers or suppliers
- Key employee risk
- Management style, corporate culture and employee relations
- Quality of facilities and equipment
- Financial obligations in outstanding leases and contracts
- Customer relations issues
- Competitive threats
- Protection of products, trademarks, brand names, sales territories
- Potential liabilities from product failures, warranties and recalls or refunds.
- Regulatory issues – taxes, legal, environmental, social and local

Any one of these risks may be significant enough to cause you to walk away from it. Note however, that many of the risks can be eliminated if you are able to buy only the assets that are of interest to you.

Unfortunately, the owners may not be interested in having you strip out the good assets as that severely reduces the value of their equity and they also lose the preferred tax treatment on capital gains from the sale.

Franchised Business

Buying into a business franchise has similar advantages and disadvantages that must be considered:

- Nature and quality of the business
- Value of the brand name
- Franchisor support, proven business model
- Franchise costs, investment costs

Most importantly, will it meet your objectives for independence, growth and profitability as an entrepreneur or will you be acting more as a passive investor or even as an employee/owner for the franchisor?

Once you have made these decisions on the structure and start-up questions, you are ready to start preparing the business plan documents and financial projections.

My recommended business plan outline and checklist are described in the following sections.

8

BUSINESS PLAN OUTLINE AND CHECKLIST

What should be in a Business Plan?

The following sections provide a complete outline and checklist of the required contents for a successful Business Plan.

The recommendations are based on my own experience, and describe the layout and content for presentation of your Business Plan. Each section lists what should be included to complete each part of your plan. You can choose your own style and format, but complete all the sections required in order to get the results you want from both the process and the document.

Be convincing, but be concise. Nobody wants to waste their time reading a long rambling presentation that does not quickly get to the point.

Typically, I recommend that your plan should be not more than 15 to 20 pages, including 3 to 5 pages of financial projections with more detail and supporting documentation placed in the appendices.

It is also important to provide a brief Executive Summary (see below) and to be able to deliver an "Elevator Pitch". (That's the 30-second to 2-minute version of your plan that you can deliver to Donald Trump when you catch him in the elevator on his way to the executive suite and want to persuade him to invest in you.)

In the following sections I describe the required contents and the recommended sequence for presentation. You can of course be creative and do it differently, but in my experience that is where you start to mess up the message. Don't make that mistake. Keep it simple.

Answer all the questions you can and don't try to bluff or B.S. your way through any of them. Recognize where your plan is weak and deal with it.

Title page

Aside from making a good first impression by presenting your business plan in a colorful glossy binder, the title page should include the name of the company, revision date, statement of purpose, prepared by whom for whom and a copy control number.

This page should also include any disclaimers (i.e. no guarantee of the forecast results, best efforts only) and provide for sign-off by the reader on your terms for confidentiality, non-disclosure, non-conflict of interest and non-compete.

All of this helps to demonstrate that you are serious and that you are a disciplined and detail-oriented manager. (Important to the reader!)

Purpose

You should include a short description of the purpose of the document on the title page or in an introductory cover note.

What are your objectives in submitting this Business Plan for review? Who is reading it and what do you expect from them?

Is it meant to attract financing, key executives, first customers or strategic partners? Is it only for internal purposes to document the corporate strategy, action plan, financial objectives and timetable?

Contents and Checklist:

The following table of contents ensures that that you will meet all of the requirements, but again you can rearrange or consolidate sections, if you are convinced that it improves the presentation of your Business Plan.

Table of Contents

The requirements for each of these sections are described below.

1. Executive Summary

This is a maximum of two to three pages, written last as a stand-alone summary document. (You may have chosen to do a draft of the executive summary to use as your initial business plan outline, but it should be revised as a final step.)

The executive summary may be offered for review prior to full disclosure of the business plan. It should be the primary "pitch" document that convinces the reader to go further, or not.

Include:

- Market opportunity
- Business concept, strategic plan and objectives
- Current status relative to the market opportunity
- Key success factors, risks, expected results
- Financial situation and needs
- Request for participation or financing

2. **Concept and Business Opportunity**

Expand on the brief Executive Summary to describe the need being addressed, how your approach is different, and why it is likely to succeed.

Include:

- Market need, customer demand and the current solutions available
- Business concept and business model or structure
- Product or service differentiation
- Initial market feedback to confirm likely success

3. **Mission, Vision, Values Statement**

Generate missionaries! Why should others join your cause – to have fun, make money, or make a difference? Where, how, for whom?

Include:

- Clear, attractive objectives – what you want to be and when.
- Statement of values and priorities for management
- Key milestones and timetable for achieving them

4. **Market Analysis**

Provide relevant, pertinent information to demonstrate your knowledge and competence in this industry.

Include:

- The overall market, recent changes
- Market segments that are attractive to you
- Target market niche and the type of customers targeted
- Customer characteristics and their needs that will make them buyers
- Buying and selling process and where you will fit in

5. Competition

Demonstrate an awareness of specific competitors and confirm your ability to compete successfully. Do not suggest that you have no competition. Your prospective customers always have choices, including ignoring you.

Include:

- Industry overview, recent trends
- Nature of competition, from inside and outside the industry
- Primary competitors – brief descriptions, compared to your concept
- Competitive products and services, relative pricing, advantages and disadvantages compared to your offering
- Competitive opportunities and their limits due to protection by patents, copyrights, other barriers to entry (theirs and yours)
- Potential competitive response – their ability to out-market, under-price, imitate or copy.

6. Strategic Plan

Describe your starting point, direction, objectives and the plan to get there.

Include:

- Company history, background and current status
- Describe experience and resources available to you
- Describe key competitive strengths and current weaknesses
- Strategy to leverage your strengths and reduce your weaknesses

Action Plan

Provide the details of key action steps in each area – organisational, operations, sales and marketing – with planned deliverables and dates for each step.

7. Management Team and Organisation Plan

This is often the most important factor in determining your success and in attracting additional staff and financing. Confidence in your business plan is based on the people responsible for it. Emphasize your current experience and competencies and your plan to fill in the gaps.

Include:

- Owner/management team, plus advisors, supporters
- Key personnel, experience and credentials
- Staffing plan and organizational structure

8. Products and Services

Consider the reader's familiarity with the industry and avoid technical jargon. Present your offering relative to the market and to what is available from current competitors.

Include:

- Product or service descriptions
- Positioning of the products and services relative to alternatives
- Competitive evaluation of products and services
- Future product and service plans

9. Marketing and Sales Plan

Marketing and sales effectiveness are essential to any successful business and must be well presented in your plan. They are too often neglected by business owners with strong professional, technical, or operations backgrounds.

Remember: Don't ever think or say out loud, "The product will sell itself".

Prepare a marketing and sales plan that will be practical, affordable and effective.

Include:

- Marketing strategy, positioning, presentation

- Confirm plans to use advertising, promotions/incentives, publicity, public relations, direct mail, trade shows, or industry events
- Describe online initiatives for Web marketing and sales
- Sales plan and tactics – use of direct sales staff, agents, distributors, or retail channels

10. Operations Plan

Describe the important issues and factors that will affect manufacturing and delivery of your products or services and the follow-up customer service and support. Define the relevant initial investments required and the ongoing operating costs.

Include:

- Description of facilities, equipment required
- Processes for product or service delivery
- Customer service and support, policy and plans
- Staffing, compensation and benefit plans

11. Risk Analysis

This is the section that deals with all the contingency plans. What can go wrong; what will you do about it? How can you prevent them or protect yourself.

Include:

- Market factors – economic cycle, interest rates, currency exchange, government regulations, trade restrictions.
- Business risks – key customer and supplier dependence, labor availability, staff turnover, new competitors, new technology and changing demand.
- Confirm contracting and legal protection, insurance plans

12. Financial Plan

Now convert all the preceding words into numbers; preferably with details of next year by month, then following three-to-five years of forecast annual results.

Include:

- Summary of business and financial assumptions in the forecasts
- Starting Balance Sheet showing initial start-up costs and planned sources of financing
- Sales, Revenue and Gross Margin forecasts
- Variable and fixed expenses
- Profit and Loss Projections
- Cash Flow Projections
- Balance Sheet Projections
- Target performance and financial ratios
- An estimate of the future value of equity

Some financial projections from an actual Business Plan are shown in the Appendix.

You may choose to show your detailed financial projections in an Appendix and extract only summary financial results for the main document. That will help to focus the reader on key numbers instead of getting lost in the details before concluding whether to proceed or not.

You can provide a summary of expected financial results with a graphic presentation, as in this example:

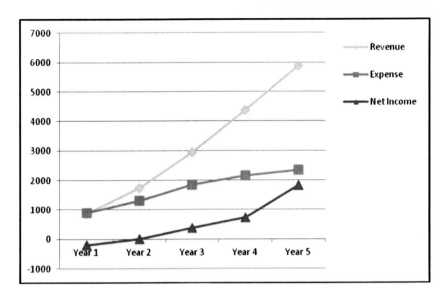

13. Conclusion

This is the final page where you ask for what you want.

Reiterate the purpose of the Business Plan and confirm what you expect from the reader. Make it clear what you are asking for and when you expect an answer. Keep it confident and enthusiastic.

Appendices to the Business plan

The Appendices are an opportunity to prove that you have done your homework and all your assumptions and forecasts are well-supported. This is also the place to add some personalization and realism to the Business Plan.

In addition to the detailed financial projections, include:

- biographies and photos of key executives
- product photos, marketing literature
- facility plans, cost estimates or quotations
- press releases, customer testimonials or letters of intent
- relevant market research documents, or published articles that support your analysis

And that completes your Business Plan!

Follow these guidelines to ensure that you have considered all the issues and that you can defend your strategies and action plans against all inquisitors. You will then have a Business Plan that is most likely to get you the response that you want from those that review it.

Maybe even the financing.

Real Life Story: "The answer – is still NO!"

This is my true story and I'm sorry, it's not very encouraging. In spite of everything I have just said about preparing a great Business Plan, you still may not get the financing you want.

In the early 2000's during the infamous Dot.com bubble, my partner and I decided to launch an e-commerce venture that was essentially a virtual distribution business for computer products. We consolidated product information from various sources in a database and then developed an online catalogue application for computer retailers with all the products showing with comparative pricing available from alternative sources. We also offered the retailers a customized storefront where they could present the same products to their customers at marked-up prices.

It may sound pretty boring now, but this was in the early days of e-commerce and online shopping. We got rave reviews from the computer distributors and retailers, "Wow, how do you do that?" Lots of users and sponsors signed up. But it was going to be costly to develop and support and we were not generating much revenue – so time to prepare a Business Plan and get the million dollar financing we needed to conquer the world.

So we did the research and prepared the documents and financial projections to support a multi-million dollar valuation and started knocking on doors. Again we got rave reviews. "Great product, great Business Plan, etc., etc."

Everything looked good for us: two experienced entrepreneurs with prior business success in the same industry; a proven business model with early customers in place; a realistic plan to build and grow the business; and reasonable projections to deliver a very high return on investment.

But the answer was still – "NO!"

Everyone had a different reason not to invest in us, but they all concluded with "Good luck and goodbye".

So we finally concluded ourselves that it was time to let it go and cut our losses. Like many other Dot.coms we went back to pursuing other career and business options.

It may happen to you. Don't be discouraged. It's just time to listen to the lessons learned and come up with a new plan. You may not have to change your goals, just the route for getting there.

9

GET THE FINANCING YOU NEED

What is the most likely source of financing? What do they want to see in your Business Plan?

With your Business Plan completed, you will now be ready to approach sources of financing. There are many alternatives available, but you will probably go through them in the following order:

- Personal investment – your own cold cash
- "Sweat equity" – personal time and effort unpaid
- "Love money" – willing friends & family
- Bank financing – term loans, lines of credit, mortgage on assets
- Angel investors – personal investors with the added value of knowledge and contacts
- Government funding, special loans, grants or subsidies
- Venture capital – private equity financing
- IPO – Initial Public Offering of shares in the business

Each of these sources will need a slightly different approach to appeal to their specific interests and concerns, but a well prepared business plan will be essential in persuading them to participate.

Very Important Note:

Before you use the business plan to request financing, be sure you can meet the one key requirement that is the most common reason for failing to get it.

Put in enough of your own cold hard cash to persuade other people to hand over theirs. Be sure you know how much is required and then prove you have more than enough.

Real Life Story: *"Things not to say out loud."*

When you are finally sitting down at the bank and reviewing your impressive and irresistible business plan, please be careful what you say.

This is not your new best friend, regardless of how friendly and helpful the banker seems; remember that they are there to avoid any risk of losing their funds and want to be sure they will make money on you.

You need to be building their confidence in the plan and your ability to deliver. I have had some clients blurt out admissions that do not help their cause with bankers, investors or potential partners.

Some real life examples:

> "We don't have any more money to put in and our mortgage loan is already at the maximum."

> "I don't really want to do this, but I lost my job and had a nervous breakdown. So it's hard to find a new job."

> "The prototype is not yet working, but I'm sure we'll get our first order soon."

> "This is obviously a multi-billion dollar market so we only need 0.002 percent market share to meet our sales projections. And the product sells itself."

> "I don't know where those numbers came from."

Try to be more discrete when you're forced to admit some of the negatives in your plan.

10

THE ENTREPRENEUR'S CHALLENGE

Once you have got your business started, the real challenge will be to successfully run a profitable and growing business. There are many opportunities to make mistakes and to stumble into unexpected problems.

From my experience, confirmed by other entrepreneurs, it is OK to occasionally fail and to make mistakes; as long as they are small and recognized early.

It's all part of the learning experience to get better. But there are some big mistakes that can kill your business.

Avoid the Seven Biggest Mistakes that Entrepreneurs Make

Here is my list of the seven biggest mistakes that entrepreneurs make and how you can avoid them.

#1 Too Entrepreneurial

Certain characteristics of entrepreneurs are necessary for them to be successful. But if over-indulged they can lead to big mistakes.

These include the tendency to be too opportunistic and not sufficiently selective and focused; to be too optimistic and miss or ignore the warning signs; to be too impatient and expect too much too soon.

Entrepreneurs usually have great confidence in their instincts and consequently rely on "gut feel". The mistake is to neglect or ignore market feedback and analysis. Being action-oriented, the tendency is to react and "fire" before the "ready, aim" stages are complete. Painful surprises can result.

Many successful entrepreneurs have achieved a lot based on their energy, charm, charisma, and persuasiveness, but then get caught continuing to sell their personality and not delivering on performance. Clients start to notice that expectations are not being met.

Entrepreneurs are expected to be decisive and demonstrate "leadership". But both can be overdone – deciding too quickly and providing too much direction so that input, initiative and creativity are stifled.

"Doing it my way" often means improvising and learning on the fly, or sticking with what works, until it stops working. The mistake is in neglecting to evolve and grow by optimizing systems and installing best practices and latest technologies.

All these mistakes can lead to serious consequences, as a result of being too entrepreneurial.

#2 Lack of Strategic Direction

Another consequence of the action-oriented entrepreneurial approach is the tendency to get lost in the daily details and completely neglect the original strategic plan and objectives.

The owner-manager soon becomes pre-occupied by operating decisions and all the demands on his time from customers, employees and the constant fire fighting. It leaves little time for fire prevention.

This situation is worsened as the entrepreneur concludes that the best solution is "do-it-myself". Not delegating to staff and not using external expertise may seem like the least-cost solution, but probably misapplies the owner's time and expertise and does not lead to long-term solutions.

The entrepreneur may have good awareness of long-term strategic issues and had them in mind when the business was launched. But they are now neglected, and the original Business Plan (if there was one) is not documented, updated or shared.

Lack of strategic direction may be the single Biggest Mistake that Entrepreneurs Make in running their businesses.

#3 "That was Easy, Let's Do It Again!"

Another common mistake that can have devastating consequences for the business is the over-confident entrepreneur who concludes, "That was easy, let's do it again!" So he or she leaps into new markets, new product lines, or even a new business or investment opportunity.

It's important to remember: Making money doesn't make you smarter.

Do you really know what you did to succeed? Or what mistakes and risks you avoided? Was it good management or good luck?

Is now a good time to start something new? How much will your current business be affected by your new initiatives?

Many successful entrepreneurs have made the mistake of jumping into a new venture – merger, acquisition, restaurant franchise or real estate investment – and blown away the equity value they generated in their original business.

It's another big mistake to avoid.

#4 Focused on Profit

Being focused on profit doesn't seem like a mistake. After all, isn't that the whole purpose of running a business?

No, actually. As I explain to students in their first Finance class, the primary financial objective of any business is "to build long-term shareholder value".

Many short-term profit-oriented decisions can hurt long-term value. The examples are many: cutting staff, maintenance or marketing expense;

not upgrading systems and technology; accepting high credit risk or low margin customers to make the extra sale; avoiding taxes; ignoring environmental or quality issues.

Most entrepreneurs are very focused on managing the bottom line by monitoring sales, gross margin and expenses. They always know those numbers.

But they are often neglecting asset management; especially cash flow. The business may appear very profitable, but have constant cash flow challenges because of poor management of inventory and receivables, in particular. And unfortunately, it is not as simple as: *"Collect Fast, Pay Slow"*. Customer and supplier relationships can be at risk, if cash flow issues force you to take that approach too aggressively.

Managing the Balance Sheet also requires good management of debt and balancing short-term and long-term needs with short-term and long-term sources of funds.

And the *Most Undervalued Asset* doesn't usually even appear on the Balance Sheet: *Human Resources*.

That leads to Biggest Mistake #5.

#5 Neglecting Key Relationships

The most important key relationship for any business is the one between owners and staff.

Management and employee communications are essential to business performance and often are not managed very well. Key employees need to be recognized and engaged. Mistakes made with key employees can jeopardize the whole business.

Similarly, don't make the mistake of being distracted by the most annoying and persistent customer. Your biggest customers are not likely the "squeakiest"; just the most important. Don't let them be neglected.

Do you need to squeak more yourself? Do your suppliers appreciate you enough?

Fast growth and profitability may be coming from one or two key customers or suppliers which can lead to your over-dependence on them. And your success may be convincing them that they don't need you in the middle any more. Be wary.

Another key relationship not to be neglected: your bank. Is your bank a welcome and willing partner in your business? Remember "friends in need" have to be developed in advance.

#6 Poor Marketing and Sales Management

You know there is a problem brewing when you hear the entrepreneur explaining that "The product sells itself"; or "Price is all that matters"; or "Our Sales Reps need to do a better job".

These are symptoms of poor marketing and sales management. Usually the company is failing at both the strategic marketing level and at the execution of effective marketing and sales programs.

Not only are opportunities for profitable growth being missed, but the company may be on the downward slide to out-of-business without a well-conceived marketing plan and effective sales strategies.

#7 Distracted by Personal Issues

Personalities and their personal issues can seriously affect business performance, regardless of whether it's the owner, management or staff. Sometimes they are simply ignored until they become a problem. Sometimes personal distractions are a result of too much success – and behaving like a rock star.

Family businesses in particular run the risk of favouritism and having family matters interfere with business success. Managing personalities and corporate culture are a particular challenge in family businesses.

That completes my list of the **Seven Biggest Mistakes that Entrepreneurs Make.**:

1. **Too Entrepreneurial**
2. **Lack of Strategic Direction**
3. **"Let's do it again!"**
4. **Focus on Profit**
5. **Neglecting Key Relationships**
6. **Poor Marketing and Sales**
7. **Personal Distractions**

How to Avoid Them? The answer is: Balance!

Each of these Big Mistakes is a result of the entrepreneur failing to achieve balance between the opposing demands on time, resources and priorities. Good choices and decisions need to be made.

Avoiding these mistakes requires the entrepreneur to:

*   Balance the Entrepreneurial Approach with Analytical Input
*   Balance Strategic Vision with Operational Detail
*   Add the Head and the Heart to the "Gut Feel"
*   Manage for Long-term Value not just Short-term Profit
*   Keep Personal Priorities in your Plan, but out of your Business

Managing to balance these issues will help you to grow and prosper in your business and avoid the *Seven Biggest Mistakes that Entrepreneurs Make.*

11

PACKAGE YOUR BUSINESS FOR SALE

Are you managing your business to maximize its value?
Sooner or later, it should be packaged for sale.

Even if your business is not for sale, you should manage like it will be someday. Are you running a business or just giving yourself a job? A real entrepreneur always manages the business to maximize its value – for the current owners and for future buyers.

It may not be a short-term objective to exit your business, but it is always a healthy management strategy to package your business as if it's for sale.

That means making it independent of you, the owner, and ensuring that the performance metrics are attractive and easily understood by outsiders. Meeting those two criteria will immediately make the business more valuable and also less demanding for you, until you are ready to exit.

It essentially means looking at your business as a dispassionate investor, instead of the emotionally committed owner. Step back and look at your business as it would appear to an outsider who is trying to put a value on it.

Remember that the value is based on only two things:

1. the expected future net income and cash flow, and
2. the degree of certainty or risk associated with achieving them.

The issues that affect the future income and cash flow are:

- Strategy, competitive positioning and branding
- Product or service plans, pricing, quality and service

- Cost control - variable and fixed
- Asset management - cash, inventory, receivables, facilities and equipment

Performance tracking and improvement efforts will require analysis of the financial ratios compared to your industry, specific competitors if possible, and checking trends over time. A future buyer, not to mention any banker or potential investor, will consider all these factors.

The issues that affect risk in the business are:

- Reliability of financial statements
- Dependence on a few customers or suppliers
- Dependence on key employees, especially the owner or family members
- Quality of management, employee relations
- Customer and supplier relationships
- Competitive threats
- Condition of facilities and equipment
- Financial obligations, loans, leases
- Protection of products, intellectual property, trademarks, brand names, territories
- Potential liabilities – product failures, warranty claims, recalls
- Regulatory issues – taxes, legal, environmental, social

You can enhance the value of your business, simply by working on increasing the returns and reducing these risks.

That usually means making the business more profitable, more stable and less dependent on you. It probably means installing a management team that can deliver the results without your direct involvement. That's a worthy benefit that will make it easier for you to exit at some point and reduce the demands on your time in the short term.

Packaging your business for sale helps you immediately to make it a better business; both more valuable and easier to manage.

12

PUT A PRICE ON YOUR BUSINESS

Maximizing your business value means knowing how to price it.

If you are managing as an owner-entrepreneur then you should be focused on maximizing the value of your business. That means understanding what determines the price. Not your ego-inflated value of the business, but the price that a dispassionate investor or buyer would put on it.

In establishing the value of your business, some basic principles must be recognized:

1. The value to the owner is unique to that individual. Ego may artificially inflate the price, but more importantly the roles and relationships established by the owner may change drastically with his or her departure, and thereby affect the price.

2. Value is always determined by an evaluation of the future income relative to the uncertainty or risks associated with obtaining the expected returns.

   Regardless of the valuation method, (P/E multiple, payback period, or discounted cash flow, described below) the forecast future income stream has to be credible and the known risks have to be reduced to get the best possible valuation.

3. Current owners tolerate more risk, uncertainty and fuzzy circumstances than new owners/investors. You may be OK with the fact that you are dependent on one key supplier because he is an old high school buddy; or that you have no signed lease, but

the landlord is your favourite uncle; or that your best sales rep is also your only son and he wants to be president.

Prospective buyers will be much less enthusiastic about these issues, unless they are all resolved to their satisfaction in advance of any offer to purchase or invest.

4. Different buyers will accept different prices, terms and conditions.

Those usually range from the passive investor looking for a reasonable return with reasonable risk; to the active investor who sees the potential to do better than your forecast under his own management; to the strategic investor who sees even greater opportunity in buying a competitor, supplier or customer and merging it with his existing business to increase revenues, eliminate unnecessary overheads, and substantially increase profits.

The selling price will depend on the perceived value seen by each of these buyers.

Several valuation methodologies may be used and it is often a good idea to test different approaches to see what values they yield and then select a selling price that can be reasonably supported by any method of valuation.

P/E Multiple

The price/earnings multiple is a well recognized valuation method and widely reported for public companies. Current price per share divided by annual earnings per share is a simple concept and a simple calculation. Unfortunately, it is not always very useful, since the selling price today is more likely based on the expectation of future earnings, not prior years' earnings.

For example, Google's share price on January 15th, 2014 was $1150 which yields a P/E multiple of 26X based on 2013 earnings estimates of $44.19 per share. But, if we use the analysts' consensus earnings estimate of $71.74 per share for 2016 then the P/E multiple is a more "reasonable" 16X. Still high compared to the less exciting Royal Bank of Canada priced at $70.90 per share with a P/E multiple of only 10.3X earnings for 2016.

What is the P/E multiple for your company?

Typically, small owner-managed businesses can support a P/E multiple ranging from 2X to 5X. It will be higher if earnings are very secure and not dependent on the current owner and management team and lower if future earnings are risky and very dependent on the current owner.

The buyer will usually look at operating income or EBITDA (Earnings before Interest, Taxes, Depreciation and Amortization) to determine profitability before financing, taxes and capital costs. That means a price of $300,000 to $500,000 on your $100,000 per year operating income, if you can agree on a P/E multiple of 3X to 5X.

Payback Period

Some buyers will insist on looking only at net cash flow and the payback period to arrive at a price. They will consider their net investment, after allowing for financing, taxes, incentives and payment terms to determine how long before they get their investment back and start earning positive cash flow. They will likely have a minimum payback period, depending on risk, ranging from 3 to 5 years.

Discounted Cash Flow

Other investors will take the financial analysts approach of calculating discounted Net Present Value (NPV) or the Return on Investment (ROI). Again the future net cash flows must be forecast to arrive at a valuation. The buyer will then discount future cash flow at the required rate of return, typically 15% to 20%, or calculate the expected ROI compared to their required rate of return. For example, the $100,000 per year cash flow on a $500,000 investment provides a 20% annual return on investment.

Using these same methods will give you a range of valuations depending on various buyer/seller scenarios to establish your own best estimate of a fair selling price.

Now you have a starting point to value your business over time. It will be useful for starting negotiations with any prospective investor or buyer and may also help in a shareholder buy-sell agreement or succession plan.

Knowing the value of your business is a key performance measure that you should be tracking regularly. The day you need to know should not be the first time you calculate it.

Real Life Story: "It's worth how much?"

Many entrepreneurs ask the question, "What is my business worth?"

I usually recommend that a simple estimate of the value be included in the financial projections for every Business Plan. The principles of valuation are well known and the math is quite simple. But the real value is established only when a buyer and seller actually agree on a price. And that depends a lot on the particular buyer and seller, their current circumstances and objectives, as illustrated by this story.

A former client with a well-established technology consulting business in Montreal called me again a few years ago to give him my assessment of the value of his business.

So I did my homework. He had over twenty years of consistent profitability, a good reputation in the industry, some proprietary software products and major international corporate accounts. All that helped the valuation multiples and lead me to estimate a value of $3 million to $3.5 million for his business.

He agreed that seemed reasonable, then said, "But I already sold it for $6 million."

"What??"

So he explained that he had accepted an offer from a big European competitor in the same industry that wanted to acquire his business for $6 million. However, he then discovered that once they owned it they planned to shut it down and move the operations into their office in Philadelphia.

That's when he said "No thanks", at any price. But he did proceed with a plan to sell equity to his key employees to ensure their loyalty (which should have been assured by his declining to cash out and kiss them goodbye).

The business continues to grow and prosper in Montreal.

Some Final Words from Uncle Ralph ... on Business Plans

Remember: Get the most out of the process.

Preparing a Business Plan will always force you to learn some things that you didn't even know you needed to know; and deliver some outputs that you hadn't expected.

For example, your Title Page will likely have a corporate name, logo and marketing slogan that you developed for your business plan. Now you can incorporate them into your business cards, brochures, e-mail signature and stationery so your business looks like it has already arrived.

You should also now have an "Elevator Pitch" and be comfortable using it: "Hello, this is who I am, what I do and why it matters to you." You should be ready for any opportunity to promote your business with the 10-second version, the two minute version, the PowerPoint slide show, the e-mail intro and the .pdf attachment.

You have probably enhanced your spreadsheet and financial analysis skills and have templates ready to assess any new changes in the industry or market landscape. Or business expansion projects with new products or new markets.

And now you've been promoted to "expert" if you, or anyone else, needs another Business Plan!

Re-Write for every Reader

Your plan needs to be written differently for different readers and different purposes. Not a substantially different plan obviously, just different emphasis and focus on what the particular reader will want to know and what you want from them.

Edit your Business Plan accordingly for each reader. It is also impressive if you personalize the cover page for each new audience.

Prior to approaching the banks or financial institutions, you should visit their websites to check their preferred business plan content and presentation. Verify if they have a particular business plan template or application form that is required. You may discover that up to a certain amount, say $100,000, they only accept applications online (avoiding wasting their time on small business clients). You may also discover that your personal financial statements and net worth are at least as important as your business plan. So get those in order and attach them to your plan.

Some readers of your plan may be more focused on your credentials and experience; others on your marketing and sales plans to support the revenue forecasts.

Submission of your Executive Summary first will help you not only gauge their interest, but also determine which questions they will be seeking answers for.

There is Never a Final Version

Your Business Plan is a working document that you should refer to regularly and review and revise annually. It was never intended for outsiders only or for one-time use only.

Of particular value for ongoing management of the business will be your financial goals, performance measures and the timetable in your Strategic Action Plan.

Continuing to monitor your progress against the plan is absolutely the best way to keep on track and achieve the objectives that you set for the business.

Remember the planning mantra: Review. Revise. Repeat.

That concludes my input to your Business Plan; the rest is up to you. *Tuum est.*

Good luck with your plans, that also helps.

Your Uncle Ralph
Del Chatterson

Appendices

Happy Pets Center Inc.

BUSINESS PLAN

(<u>Note</u>: Actual client names and numbers have been changed to protect their confidentiality.)

Purpose:

This Business Plan documents the strategies and plans for expansion of **Happy Pets Center Inc.** to provide potential investors and sources of financing with the information required to evaluate the business opportunities and financial requirements associated with this expansion plan.

Prepared By:	David Howe, President, **Happy Pets Center Inc.**
Assisted By:	Del Chatterson, DIYBusinessPlan.com

acknowledges that he/she has no conflicting personal or business interests in any way related to pet care or veterinary services.

Copy # _____

Accepted and receipt acknowledged by: _____

Signed _____

To the reader:

Thank you for your interest in our Business Plan which presents the strategies and plans for the expansion of our business. Please note that it is a confidential document between us and subject to the terms of the Non-Disclosure Agreement attached as Appendix A.

We are asking you to review this Business Plan for the purpose of your considering participation in financing the expansion of Happy Pets. The business has been financed to date by the current shareholders and internal cash flow. Full realization of the business opportunities attainable through expansion will require additional financing as described in this Business Plan.

Please contact us directly if you have further questions or wish to arrange a follow -up meeting after reviewing the Business Plan. We appreciate your interest in our plans.

Yours truly,

David Howe, President.

Happy Pets Center Inc.
BUSINESS PLAN

TABLE OF CONTENTS:

APPENDICES:

1. Executive summary

Happy Pets Center Inc. currently operates a storefront business on AAA Street in West Town and is planning to expand its facilities and services to a larger pet center. The new pet center will be an easily accessible destination located in the South Park area with about 9000 sq. ft. including a retail space for pet nutrition, supplies and accessories, a veterinary clinic for diagnosis and treatment of pets and additional facilities for pet grooming.

The Happy Pets approach has been developed and proven over the last 3-1/2 years and demand for our services continues to grow. The current facility is stretched beyond its capacity and other retailers are expanding their services to respond to the opportunities. It is timely for Happy Pets to build on its established credibility and maintain its leadership position.

The new facility will require additional financing of approximately $235,000 over the next four to six months for the necessary capital equipment, leasehold improvements and start-up expenses. This new Happy Pets Pet Center is expected to achieve satisfactory profitability within two years at a projected revenue of $2 million per year.

The following Business Plan provides more details on the business concept, strategy, operating plans and financial projections.

2. Concept and business opportunity

Happy Pets Center Inc. is a business dedicated to promoting and supporting the care of domestic family pets. Our approach to pet care is growing in importance as consumers and pet owners become more aware of the requirements for adequate pet care and of the difference that good care can make to owning healthier and happier family pets.

Currently, Happy Pets operates a small retail outlet on AAA Street in West Town offering pet nutrition and accessory products, grooming services and limited veterinary care. This storefront operation opened in late 2006 and has demonstrated the growing demand for healthy and ethical pet nutrition products and services.

This Business Plan addresses the opportunity for an expanded pet center in a new facility. The new center will be in a more accessible location allowing it to become the regional destination for quality pet care. It will attract and be able to serve a much larger clientele. It will continue to focus on high quality natural pet nutrition products and services. It will also offer a wide range of complementary products and services including health remedies, food diets, supplements, pet accessories and supplies, grooming services, and limited veterinary care.

Market demand for Happy Pets type of pet care is growing with the trends to increasing consumer demand for natural food and health care products and with the increasing public awareness of issues related to the proper care and treatment of their animals. These issues receive continuous attention in the media – product safety, animal testing, use of chemicals and additives in food products, inadequate health and safety standards. Just as consumers become more demanding for their own health and well-being they also recognize the importance of these issues in the care and nutrition of their pets. Although major name brand suppliers continue to supply pet shops with their generic pet foods, they have recognized the growing consumer demand and are responding effectively

Happy Pets is very focused on catering to the needs for natural pet nutrition and healthy pet care by providing better information, products and services than any other pet care store in Canada. The principals in Happy Pets have well recognized reputations for their expertise and integrity in pet care and this distinguishes them from any competitor. Pet care products are available from a wide variety of sources – high volume national retailers to the local pet shop. But no one else can offer the level of expertise and dedication to healthy pet care that are available from Happy Pets.

This combination of growing demand and lack of credible suppliers presents a continuing business opportunity that must be addressed by Happy Pets before a direct competitor can establish itself in the target market. Customer demand for products and services at the existing Happy Pets outlet already exceeds the capacity of the store. More space, expanded inventory, additional facilities and services combined with easier access and parking will allow the business to support demand from the metropolitan area and beyond. An effective marketing campaign will quickly build traffic to the new location and deliver sales revenues in line with our projections.

The Business Plan for expansion addresses this business opportunity and demonstrates the profit potential for investors. Our objective is to grow from current sales of approximately $300,000 per year at the current store to achieve additional sales at an expanded pet center exceeding $2,000,000 per year within three years. We will achieve these goals by maintaining a dedication to healthy pet care and providing a complete range of products and services that meet consumer demands.

3. **Mission statement**

Happy Pets is committed to becoming the Canadian leader in healthy pet care. The company's mission is to:

- Educate – creating awareness of healthy choices in pet nutrition and care.
- Prevent – providing products and services to ensure the long term well-being of pets.
- Heal – offering a basic range of veterinary services to cure pet ailments.

Adherence to these principles will guide the business stategies and operating practices of Happy Pets in its expansion plans.

4. **Market analysis**

MARKET OPPORTUNITY

American pet food sales were $13.64 billion in 2004. Manufacturers' sales growth was 3.6% in 2003 over 2002. Organic pet food sales were estimated at $32 million in 2004 and growing. (Ref.: *Pet Age*, February 2005.)

The IAMS Company, owned by Procter & Gamble has global sales of $1.3 billion in 70 countries and is the No. 1 brand name in the United States. The company has grown from its start in 1950 by focusing on higher quality pet nutrition. Other pet food manufacturers are also catering to higher quality demands and developing products for more specific pet requirements.

In spite of generally poor retail sales at the end of 2004, the pet industry had more positive results. Two large U.S. retailers, PETCO and PetsMART had third quarter sales increases of 7.0% and 6.7%. Pet owners continue to spend generously on their animals with annual expanditures of $416 per year by cat owners and $475 per year by dog owners according to a 2003-2004 APPMA National Pet Owners Survey in the U.S.

The survey indicates that 40% of that spending goes on pet food. 35% of pet owners shop in supermarkets and spend an average of $8.99 to $14.99 for a 20-lb. bag of dog food. Premium brands are selling at $35.00 per 40-lb. bag. Pet owners also spend an average of $50 (Minimum of $45 for small dogs, up to $90 for large dogs) per grooming, $20-$30 per day for daycare, and costs for veterinary services run from $100 per visit for fees and remedies up to to several hundreds, even thousands of dollars, for tests, medication, surgery and follow-up care. (Ref.: *Pet Business*, February 2005.)

Pet retailers have recognized the business expansion opportunities of catering to pet owners needs and are introducing additional services such as grooming, daycare, pet walking, training classes, and pet tharapy. Their efforts also include building brand loyalty and demonstrating social responsibility by participating in adoption clinics, animal welfare events and contributing to animal rescue organisations.

The concept of providing healthier natural pet care initiated by Happy Pets is starting to be imitated by some new local competitors: Big Doggy (2 stores), masters Pet (3 stores), Bark and Meow (a new franchise), and also some existing stores: Three Bears, Klub K-9 and Martin Pets. Their intiatives help to confirm the interest in healthier pet care services and reinforce the strategy of protecting our leadership position by taking the concept to the next level with a larger integrated pet center.

Previous analysis of the Canadian pet care market in our Business Plan of 2001 indicated Canadian pet care spending averaging approximately $400 per year on 4.5 million cats and 3.5 million dogs in Canada. (*StatsCan – 1999.*) Based on a regional population of at least 3.5 million in the area served by the new pet center, and assuming the same spending per year and the same ratio of pets to total population (8/30 million), the total pet care market in the region is estimated at $373 million per year. If 5% of that market is seeking natural, premium grade products and healthier pet care, then the total market potential for Happy Pets is $18.65 million.

We are confident that the new Happy Pets Pet Center can achieve satisfactory profitability and return on investment at $2,000,000 in sales which would represent an estimated 10.7% market share within two years.

TARGET MARKETS

Pet owners who are concerned about animal health and welfare and have a preference for natural products and a healthy approach to care, prevention and treatment are the most relevant prospective customers for Happy Pets. These pet owners currently represent about 5% of total Canadian spending on pet nutrition and health care.

Customer needs

Customer characteristics that favour Happy Pets are the need for information, integrity, and consistency in the offering of healthy natural products and pet care services. These are the competitive advantages of Happy Pets.

Buying process

Customers have found Happy Pets through various means – walk by traffic, press coverage, follow-up to magazine articles and referrals from veterinarians, health practitioners and health food stores.

As they become aware of the issues, pet care alternatives and the availability of the Happy Pets Center pet owners become customers, then advocates and strong referral sources by word-of-mouth marketing.

The choice of a new location with easy highway access and adequate free parking will make the pet centre a regional destination for all healthy pet care needs. (Public transit is less important.)

5. Competition

The U.S. market is dominated by two national chains, PETSCO and PetsMART with a total of 1400 outlets and combined sales exceeding $5 billion. Both chains are expanding rapidly and expected to win customers and sales volume from both independent retailers and the supermarkets. Industry experts expect that the smaller, regional chains will be most vulnerable to the powerful economies of scale while the owner-operated specialty retailer will be able to retain customers with a closer personal touch and focused product lines.

The third largest pet retailer is Pet Value of Markham Ontario with 350 outlets in Ontario and Manitoba and the U.S. Mid Atlantic region. About 120 units are franchisees and most are located in 1200 to 2500 sq. ft. near a neighbourhood shopping mall. None of the larger franchises are yet in Quebec, deterred by the usual language and cultural issues, but they are likely to be present soon given the size of the Quebec market and the lack of high profile branded competitors.

Petcetera is another growing and successful pet retailer in Canada opening in Vancouver in 1997 and now operating 37 stores in five provinces. They are also dedicated to animal welfare and provide services to support animal adoption of 500 – 800 dogs and cats per month. In the interest of animal welfare they do not sell live dogs, cats or exotic pets.

Most independent pet retailers try to offer a full range of products. None have the integrity and dedication to natural/healthy/ethical products that will continue to distinguish Happy Pets from its competitors. Furthermore, Happy Pets is known and recognized by its retail peers, local veterinarians and the public for having the professional expertise and experience that sets it apart as Canada's leader in complete healthy pet care.

The current most significant competitors to Happy Pets are:

- ABC .... established for many years, it would appear to be comparable to Happy Pets in the type of products, size and style of operation, and type of clientele. Not conveniently or centrally located it is probably limited to the local residential area of pet owners.

- Bark & Meow, an Ontario franchise, just recently opened, its success is not yet established.
- Three Bears, owned by two women partners, who are its second owners, they have a reputation for poor customer service and lack of expertise. They are not expected to survive.
- CDK ... In operation for at least eight years by its original owners, their sales probably rival those of Happy Pets. Their product lines and setup are similar to those of Three Bears, although their store is approximately three times the size.

As Happy Pets has succeeded in the local market, its competitors have responded with the addition of "natural" products to their inventory. But these competitors will require time or large promotional expenditures to establish their credibility and build customer awareness.

Competition at various levels will continue to exist from the full range of national retailers, local pet shops, private groomers and pet therapists, and traditional veterinarians. However, the unique positioning and competitive strengths of Happy Pets will allow us to retain significant market share, grow and build a successful, profitable business.

6. **Strategic plan**

BUSINESS HISTORY

Founded by David Howe and partners, the current storefront was opened September 10, 2005. Since then, it has established a loyal and enthusiastic clientele and built solid relations with key suppliers. (See testimonials in Appendix J)

Ownership and Management

Happy Pets Center, Inc. is a legal entity incorporated under the province of Quebec in 2005. It is currently owned 100% by David Howe. A plan is in place to have the other key members of the management team, acquire up to 10% each in the new business, prior to the issuing of additional shares to any major new investor(s). A binding contract between all three parties will be drawn to ensure a lasting and exclusive business relationship.

Intellectual Property Protection

No current products or processes have been developed that require protection by patent or copyright. The company name is in the process of being trademarked for the potential use of "Happy Pets" on future branded products.

REGULATORY ISSUES / CERTIFICATIONS

In order to operate a veterinary clinic, that part of the business must be under the ownership and control of a registered veterinarian. Pet groomers do not require any specific certification or licencing. Other standard retail business licencing requirements will be met in the new location.

Current strategic position

Happy Pets is seen by customers, competitors and suppliers as a strong advocate and knowledgeable source for natural pet care products and healthy treatment of pets. That reputation adds credibility and brand value to the new pet center.

STRATEGIC OBJECTIVES:

Following are the key strategic objectives for the expansion plan:

1. Establish sustainable and profitable businesses processes at the current store to achieve annual sales of $500,000, adequate return to the owner, and net income of $30,000 per year by September 30, 2005.
2. Complete negotiations for new equity and debt financing to support the expansion plan by June 30, 2005.
3. Complete the expansion project to open the new Pet Center premises by October 31, 2005.
4. Achieve sustainable annual sales at the new Pet Center of $1,500,000 per year by September 30, 2006.
5. Achieve annual sales at the new Pet Center of $2,500,000 per year by September 30, 2009 with net profit after tax of $150,000 per year.
6. Open two new storefront operations (franchised or owned); one by March 2006, and another by September 2006.
7. Expand distribution rights for selected nutrition products to achieve annual distribution sales exceeding $100,000 per year by September 30, 2008.
8. Begin research and development for production of Happy Pets lines of pet food and supplements by January 2009.

Strategic Action Plan:

1. Make initial presentations of the Business Plan to bank lendors and potential new investors by March 31, 2005.
2. Identify the preferred sources of financing and confirm the general arrangements by May 31, 2005.
3. Finalize negotiations for financing and initiate the plans for leasing new premises by June 30, 2005.
4. Complete the leasehold improvements and installation of capital equipment to open the new Pet Center by October 31, 2005.
5. Develop and launch a marketing plan that coincides with the opening of the new Pet Center and drives initial traffic to the new location.
6. Manage the Pet Center to deliver the forecast revenues and profits.

7. Management team

A primary competitive strength of Happy Pets arises from the combined knowledge, skills and experience of its management team. The key members who are dedicated to achieving the company's objectives are:

David Howe, President

He is a well-known and respected authority on pet products, healthy pet care and the ethical treatment of animals. He is a regular contributor to a variety of publications on these subjects. He also has experience in sales and marketing of natural pet nutrition products prior to opening Happy Pets and has been active in promoting and managing the current retail store to ensure its profitable growth since opening in 2001.

Mr Smooth

... is a trained and experienced pet groomer as well as an active supporter of pet welfare. He has been active in providing pet grooming services at Happy Pets since March, 2003. He has also assisted in the physical setup of the current location.

Background information and the credentials of each of these individuals are provided in more detail in Appendix D along with an initial organizational structure. Additional experienced resources are known to the management team and will be engaged as required.

The organizational plan and the associated staffing costs are presented with the financial schedules of Appendix C .

8. Product and service offering

The new pet center will allow expansion of the products and services already available from the current storefront on AAA Street.

Pet Nutrition:

- Certified, all natural, high qualitypet food.
- Dietary supplements.
- Veterinary remedies

Pet supplies and accessories:

- Leashes, beds, bowls
- Pet clothing
- Souvenirs, cards, calendars
- Books and magazines

Pet care products:

- All natural shampoos
- Hygeine products
- Natural, non-toxic household cleaning products.

Pet care services:

- grooming
- behavioral therapy
- Tharapeutic pet massage

Healthy veterinary services:

- acupuncture and acupressure
- Chiropractic
- physiotherapy

FUTURE PRODUCTS AND SERVICES

Happy Pets is in constant growth and development for both new products and services. These include foods, accessories, and services. Although we currently cover all possible healthy pet care services, there is the potential to add pet day care, hotel-style boarding and dog walking.

9. **Marketing and sales plan**

The marketing strategy for Happy Pets Healthy Pet Center will be targeted on the specific market niche of pet owners interested in natural products for nutrition and healthy treatments for pet care.

The positioning strategy will emphasis the integrity and qualifications of Happy Pets in the field of healthy pet care. It will emphasize the knowledge and experience advantages of Happy Pets over other sources of pet nutrition and healthy pet care. The management team will continue to be active in advocacy and public relations for natural pet nutrition, healthy treatment and the ethical treatment of animals. The strong media interest in these subjects has provided good exposure for Happy Pets in the past. (See Appendix K.)

To maintain our competitive advantage, sales and service staff will be screened to ensure their attitudes and interests are in line with the mission of Happy Pets. Training will provide them with the necessary knowledge to help inform customers and assist in their pet care decisions.

A limited number of products will be sold and they will continue to be carefully selected from suppliers that meet our criteria for high quality, natural products and ethical business practices.

Advertising and promotion activities for the new pet center will include health and pet oriented publications and events more than the general media. The company and its management team will be active in sponsorship and participation for SPCA activities, pet adoption, and by organizing fund raising events for pet shelters in various boroughs.

A strong referral network will be built with local veterinary clinics and health food stores to direct interested customers to Happy Pets. Appropriate marketing materials will be made available to these locations. Some incentive programs may need to be developed to encourage these sources of referrals.

Pet industry trade shows and other industry events will be attended to promote Happy Pets both locally and internationally and to develop important relationships with other participants in healthy pet care.

10. **Operations plan**

LOCATION AND FACILITIES

Happy Pets is currently located on AAA Street in West Town. Since it is the only pet supply store in the region dedicated to natural pet nutrition and healthy pet care with such strong qualifications, expertise and credibility, it draws customers from many miles away. Inquiries for access to our unique products and servicse have been received from across Canada, the U.S. and the U.K.

A review of the current active customer list indicates a particularly large distribution of customers from the South Park area. This factor has influenced the interest in selecting a new location in South Park.

The new facility is planned for approximately 8000 - 9000 square feet of space with about 4000 sq. ft. dedicated to the retail store, 1300 for the veterinary clinic, 1200 sq. ft. for for grooming. A small office will be required at about 150 sq. ft., a small kitchenette with two tables at about 250-300 sq. ft. Obedience/dog training classes or hosting other courses/activities, will need an area designated for such purposes; aproximately 600-800 square feet. Additional space for washrooms and common areas indicate a minimum requirement of about 8000 sq. ft. An initial general layout of the facilities is provided in Appendix H.

Operating Processes

The retail portion of the new pet center will be open for normal operating hours of Monday to Wednesday 9:00am – 6:00pm; Thursday and Friday 9:00am – 9:00pm; Saturday and Sunday 10:00am – 5:00pm. The clinic will be open Monday to Friday from 9:00am to 7:00pm.

Staffing will include well-trained and motivated retail sales clerks compensated with appropriate base salaries and a shared commission plan for additional incentive.

Mr. Smooth will manage the groomers as independent contractors paid on a per cent of fees earned. He will also be charged a monthly allocation for the use of premises.

Current suppliers will be retained and the new facility will make it easier to accommodate and expand the distribution business for resale of selected product lines to other pet retailers. This could become more significant if addressed as a separate business opportunity but will require additional investment to do so.

For many current customers the new facility will be much more convenient to access and pick up products. Sales volume per customer should increase accordingly. The existing store may see some sales decline but costs can be offset by reducing the hours of service. It is also expected that the marketing programs will have a spillover effect and drive new traffic to the existing store. It will remain a model and test location for other storefront operations.

11.   Risk analysis

The investment risks are understood and will be managed to the minimum possible. These risks arise from both market or economic conditions that are not controllable by Happy Pets and from business conditions that are internal to Happy Pets.

Market risks:

1. Decline of overall market.

    Trends do not suggest any likely decline of the overall market for pet supplies. Risk to Happy Pets is limited by its relatively small but growing market share and its ability to compensate for any general market decline by increasing its market share.

2. New competitor.

    Potential exists for a new competitor but Happy Pets has the opportunity to create a market leadership position in its chosen niche of healthy pet care.

3. New market requirements.

    It is unlikely that the trends toward natural products and healthy health care will suddenly shift to new approaches. This is not a short-term fashion or fad concept.

Business risks:

1. Availability of key personnel

    Happy Pets will offer opportunities for profit participation as an incentive to retain key management staff and also have signed employment contracts that provide protection from abrupt termination by either party. Operating employees will not be unionized so mass withdrawal of services is unlikely.

2.   Loss of suppliers

Protection of supply will be achieved by negotiated contract terms and by maintaining alternative sources.

3.   Systems and facilities risks

Happy Pets will take reasonable precautions to protect systems and facilities and also maintain commercial insurance against business interruption.

3.   Regulatory

Happy Pets will maintain and upgrade all regulatory approvals as necessary.

The financial projections show that Happy Pets's business model has strong revenue potential that is attractive in spite of these normal business risks.

12.   **Financial plan**

A detailed financial plan is attached as Appendix A.

The Financial Plan includes the following:

A.   Summary of financial results to date for the current store.
B.   Financial projections for the current store
C.   Financial Forecasts for the expanded Healthy Pet Center:

- Opening Balance Sheet and Financial Requirements
- Capital Expenditures and Leasehold Improvements
- Sales Revenue and Gross Profit Projections
- Organisation Plan
- Expense Forecast
- Net Income and ROI Projections
- Cash Flow Forecast
- Investment Forecast
- Projected Balance Sheets

This Business Plan has been prepared to describe the business opportunity, the strategy, the operating plan, and the expected financial results. Thank you for your interest in reviewing it.

- - - - - - - -

Appendix C: Financial Plan - Notes to Financial projections:

1. Start-up costs are detailed in the attached schedule of capital expenditures and leasehold improvements. Assumed future expenditures are simply estimates of expansion needs for upgrades and replacements.

2. Schedule 1: Revenue projections are based on the sales factors applied to each revenue category for the periods indicated. Pet nutrition is the primary revenue generator at approximately 57% of total annual sales. The relationship between revenue categories shown in the monthly sales factors is based on current experience.

3. Sales per square foot for pet food and accessories is $268 per square foot in the new retail pet center versus $237per sq. ft. in the current store.

4. Grooming services are estimated at $50 per hour with two groomers working 20 hours per week to generate $8000 per month in Year 1. Each groomer will average four groomings per day.

5. Therapy services are estimated at an average $70/hour ($40 minimum ½ hour and $60/hour). The area is forecast to be used 4 hours per day, 4 days per week in the first year for 64 hours per month and $4480 in revenue.

6. Veterinary services are estimated to generate average fees of $115 per hour and average billings of six hours per day per vet. We have assumed one veterinarian available at 120 hours per month, plus another junior vet or technician available 40 hours per month generating the same average fee rate. Veterinary care products have historically generated revenue at 50% of the veterinary fees.

7. Distribution revenue is currently a small part of the business and is forecast to grow to only $200,000 per year within five years. This may be addressed as a separate business opportunity.

8. The start-up phase of three months in the new pet center is estimated to generate approximately two months of normal revenue.

9. Year 2 nutrition revenue is estimated to grow at 30% over Year 1 with subsequent years growing at 15%. Other categories are forecast to grow proportionally. Revenue estimates do not include any provision for inflation or escalation of fee rates and do not include sales taxes collected or paid.

10. Gross margin calculations are based on historical costs for products, services and selling expenses from prior years. Veterinarians and groomers are paid at 85% and 50% of their fees, respectively. The veterinary clinic

will also pay rent for the premises as indicated in the expense deduction of Schedule 3.

11. Schedule 2: Staffing costs are based on the full-time employee equivalent hours and the salary rates as indicated. Benefits are estimated at 15% over base salaries. The management team is included in these costs at estimated market values for the services provided by each. Retail sales staff are increased in the third year and staff for distribution are added when sales reach $100,000 per year.

12. Schedule 3: Overhead and administrative expenses are estimated at 10% of staff costs. Rent on the new pet center has been estimated at $11.00 p.s.f. gross rate on 9000 sq. ft. ($99,000 per year, $8250 per month, escalating at 3% per year.) Recent quotations on available premises range from $9.00 to $14.00 per sq. ft. depending on the quality of the premises and the location. Other annual expenses are in line with current operating costs.

13. Schedule 4: Net income before tax is calculated after depreciation and financing charges. Taxes are estimated at 18% of net income.

14. Schedule 5: Cash flow projections are based on sales receipts being collected in the same month as the sale. Most sales will be cash or credit card. Credit card discounts have not been included. The cash flow impact of sales taxes collected and paid has not been included as the net effect is near zero. Product costs and operating expenses are projected to be paid in the same month they are incurred.

15. Income taxes are shown as paid at year-end. No dividends are projected in the first five years.

16. The assumed cash flow projections show a need for increased equity financing of $125,000 and corresponding bank loans increasing to $125,000 by the end of Year 1. Loans can subsequently be paid down to meet only the ongoing working capital requirements.

17. Schedule 6: Investment requirements are shown for inventory, receivables at zero (cash only) and capital equipment expenditures and carried forward to the projected Balance Sheets.

18. Schedule 7: Balance Sheet projections show the estimated future assets and liabilities and the growth in Retained Earnings without any dividend payments.

GO Freight Inc.

BUSINESS PLAN

Purpose:

This Business Plan documents the strategies and plans for **GO Freight Inc**. The primary purpose of this document is to provide potential investors and sources of financing with the information required to evaluate the risks and opportunities associated with this business.

Prepared By: ….., President,

Revised: January 8, 2014
….., Vice-President, Marketing
Copy # _____

GO FREIGHT INC.

Website: www.companyx.com

Assisted By: Del Chatterson, Consultant

<u>Disclaimer:</u> The management and owners of this business and our consultants make no warranties or representations as to the validity of facts, forecasts and assumptions, or the viability of this plan. The reader is solely responsible for any conclusions or decisions based on the information herein.

<u>Confidentiality and Non-Conflict of Interest</u>: This business plan contains information that is confidential to GO Freight and its owners. It is not to be shared or copied without their prior consent. The reader further acknowledges that he/she has no conflicting personal or business interests in any way related to the planned products or services of GO Freight.

Accepted and receipt acknowledged by:

_____

Signed

_____

Name   Title

_____   _____

Company: Date

To the reader:

Thank you for your interest in our Business Plan.

In it we present the strategies and plans for the expansion of our business and it must be treated as a confidential document between us.

We are asking you to review this Business Plan for the purpose of your considering participation in the financing of GO Freight. The initial financing of the business has been provided by the current shareholders. Full realization of the business opportunities available will require additional financing as described in this Business Plan.

We appreciate your interest in our plans. Please contact us directly if you have further questions or wish to arrange a follow-up meeting after reviewing the Business Plan.

Yours truly,

President
GO FREIGHT INC.

GO FREIGHT

BUSINESS PLAN

TABLE OF CONTENTS:

APPENDICES:

13. Executive summary

GO Freight is a new freight services company being launched by two experienced industry professionals with excellent credentials and industry contacts that are already prepared to do business with the new company.

The trucking industry in our area is frequently showing poor levels of performance and customer service and local shippers are ready to consider new alternatives. This situation is creating the opportunity for GO Freight with its knowledge, experience, and contacts to successfully deliver better shipping performance and better customer service. GO Freight will offer traffic management solutions for full truckload shipments, including domestic, import/export, refrigerated trucks, and flat-bed trucks.

GO Freight will focus on delivering services that are cost effective with dependable performance and high levels of customer service. GO Freight will provide transportation management services including the following:

- Analysis of traffic patterns to determine specific handling requirements.
- Developing least-cost solutions to meet the shipper's needs.
- Contracting with the appropriate carriers that will meet the desired service levels for our customers.

The company forecasts sales of $3.4 million in freight revenue in the first year, growing to at least $5 million within five years. Financial projections show this to be a very profitable business opportunity.

In addition to the initial equity investment of $30,000 from the two shareholders, initial bank financing of up to $60,000 is required to support working capital needs, but it is expected to be fully repaid within the first full year of operation.

14. Concept and business opportunity

GO Freight is a new freight services company offering traffic management solutions for overland transportation. This service is known in the freight business as a "third party logistics" company and provides outsourced transport services for a wide variety of shippers requiring inbound and outbound freight services.

GO Freight will focus on delivering specific transportation services that are more effective and economical with higher levels of customer service than companies are otherwise receiving from their internal traffic department or from direct contracting with the trucking companies.

The trucking industry is currently in turmoil due to a variety of factors including the declining manufacturer shipping volumes, the high costs of fuel and consolidation or downsizing among current carriers. The consequence of these distractions for truckers is that both operating performance and customer service are suffering. The effects are evident in missed deliveries, poor customer relations, and low levels of satisfaction for shippers. These conditions are creating an opportunity for our company with the knowledge, experience, and contacts to successfully deliver better shipping performance and better customer service. This is the opportunity being pursued by GO Freight.

The principal owner/managers of GO Freight, ..., and ...., have the necessary expertise and combined experience of more than 30 years in the trucking industry. They know the major shippers and carriers operating in our region and how service and performance can be improved for both parties. Initial feedback from prospective customers that are under-served and carriers that are under-utilized is already very encouraging. (See Testimonials in Appendix ....)

GO Freight see its role of providing expertise and transportation management services to major shippers including the following:

- Analysis of traffic patterns to determine specific handling requirements.
- Developing least-cost solutions to meet the shipper's needs.
- Contracting with the appropriate carriers to meet the desired service levels.

GO Freight will also provide sales representation for carriers from outside our region who do not have representation here to sell their services to local shippers. These carriers are already delivering into the region and have space available for low cost back-hauls that GO Freight can fill effectively and increase their revenues while also delivering cost savings to the shippers.

Specific target markets have been identified that are likely to have stable demand, are generally profitable businesses, and have reasonably complex requirements that offer cost saving opportunities. These industries include:

- Fresh and frozen food products
- Horticultural products
- Health care products
- Seasonal products

GO Freight will initially limit itself to offering road freight services for full loads, but these will include domestic, import/export, refrigerated trucks, and flat-bed trucks.

An initial forecast for the first full-year indicates a sales potential exceeding $3.4 million based on known customer prospects and their current shipping volumes. Growth in the second year should be at least 20% and then continue to a level of at least $5 million within five years. Financial projections show this to be a very profitable business opportunity and a secure credit risk.

Initial financing will be required in the form of a line of credit to support working capital needs in addition to the initial equity investment of $30,000 from the two shareholders. The total bank financing requirement is expected to rise to an amount of $60,000 during the first two quarters, but is expected to be fully repaid within the first full year of operation.

15. Mission, Vision, Values

GO Freight is committed to becoming recognized as the premier specialist in road transportation for major shippers in our region that require non-standard freight services.

We see ourselves as offering unique expertise and experience that will allow our customers to benefit from cost reductions in their overland freight while receiving exceptional levels of customer service unmatched by our competitors.

GO Freight is also committed to maintaining strong loyalty and dedication from the carriers it uses based on our consistent respect for their requirements, including fair compensation and prompt payment for their services.

Our approach to the market will be through our extensive contact network leveraging our reputations for integrity, competence and dedication to meeting our customers' requirements.

Our approach to management of the business incorporates the principals associated with owner/management and long-term growth of a profitable enterprise. We are dedicated to being successful for our customers, carriers, and employees.

16. Market analysis

The Transportation Market

Supply chain management can be described as supplying the correct product or service, to the correct place, in the correct quantity, at the correct time and at the correct cost.

The National Logistics .... Study, of March 2008, found that supply chain costs represent 32% of the total of manufactured products.

Furthermore, 75% of national corporations of all sizes are encountering difficulty hiring highly qualified logistics personnel, hence the need for outsourcing to experienced logistics managers who can plan and control the efficient movement of goods between shipper and consignee on their customers' behalf. In 2007, the top outsourced supply chain activities were customs brokerage and clearance, freight forwarding, inbound and outbound transportation and warehousing.

In the Logistics / Supply Chain .... National Overview (Sept 2008), research showed that logistics users generally outsourced transportation: 73% of firms outsourced their inbound transportation and 68% outsourced their outbound transportation. Transportation accounts for 85% of the logistics industry revenues estimated at $50 billion. Trucking was the key sub-sector with 42% of the whole logistics industry and 75% of the transportation sector.

This sub-sector is stable and starting to have some differentiation factors due to just-in-time (JIT), and enhanced client demands regarding technology integration. The single greatest potential challenge to the trucking sector in recent history was during the aftermath of the September 11 terrorist attacks in the United States. While inconveniencing cross-border transportation for a number of weeks, the final impact has been more complex and time consuming security procedures that require more expertise and the application of new technology for border crossing truckers.

Target Sectors

GO Freight will focus on this trucking sub-sector and, more specifically, on the full truck-load business. We feel that this strategy will enable us to avoid the distractions commonly encountered by those who enter the market with a wider service offering . Our initial target customers are all financially solid players in stable markets themselves.

The major accounts currently contacted within our target market, our potential revenue rand their total transport business are shown in the table below:

Company	Total Freight Value	% Potential	Revenue Potential for GO Freight
Fruit Co	$$$$	X %	$$$
Health Foods Inc.			
XYZ Medical			
Others Inc.			

Customer needs

Customer needs are well understood by the principals of GO Freight and they are also aware of the current deficiencies in performance and customer service. Focusing on meeting those needs, while delivering lower transportation costs, will assure us of attracting, retaining and growing key customer accounts. Maintaining strong, loyal customer relationships is a key element in the sales management plan.

Buying process

In most cases, after an introduction to the services of GO Freight, the shipper will provide enough information on traffic patterns and handling requirements to evaluate their needs and develop a proposal for services. This proposal will be submitted with recommended carriers, routes and the associated costs for comparison by the buyer to current procedures or to alternative submissions. If GO Freight is successful in being the chosen solution then shipping orders will be confirmed by fax, e-mail or telephone.

17. **Competition**

Third party logistics is a well established industry offering a variety of services to large multi-nationals and smaller regional companies. The services vary from small package pick-up and delivery to specialty trucking, air and ocean freight, brokerage, warehousing or full logistics management.

Industry characteristics

These services are provided by a wide range of potential competitors for GO Freight. There are large full service companies with a global presence down to local specialists with limited staff and capabilities.

Primary Competitors

Some recognized competitors and their relative market positions are described below:

1. ABC Transport

Started : 1995
Major services: transport, warehousing and distribution
Size: over $10 million in sales

Wide use of technologies including satellite tracking on all company trucks, EDI introduced in January 2001, and other technologies being considered.

Service is not consistent or necessarily better because of the technologies. Their service has become so diversified that the fundamentals are being lost, and the latest technologies are not being used to help serve their customers.

2. XYZ Freight

25 years in business
Services include: (in order)
Full-Service Transportation Logistics Carrier and Agency Network

Again, very diversified. Has broken into the LTL market in the past year alone.

3. Logistics Co. Int'l.

Established 1993
Logistics management and warehousing services

Specialize in supplier management, material inventory and procurement and warehousing.

4. Traffic Co.

Established 1986
Very customer-centric. Reps available 24 hours a day by cell.
Latest technologies. Divisions started by specializing in vertical

markets but have combined into the traditional refrigerated, rail, warehousing,

Probably strongest competition for GO Freight.

5. Logistics Company Inc.

Started 1989.
Started in freight brokering but have added many other services over the years:

In addition to these third party logistics companies, many shippers will assume responsibility themselves and contract directly with individual transport companies. Competition from all these options is recognized and respected. Sometimes customers will remain loyal to their current logistics service providers and some competitors will offer services that GO Freight does not. In these circumstances, there may be no potential business for us.

Nevertheless, our competitors all have weaknesses that lead to performance deficiencies, communications breakdowns and deterioration of customer relationships. These situations all present business opportunities for GO Freight. Our own established customer contacts, our reputation for effective service delivery, and our dedication to constant communication with the customer will allow us to consistently win new business. By focusing on full truckload services and not over-extending our resources, we expect to protect and retain these competitive advantages and build strong, long-term customer relationships with major shippers in our target markets.

18. Strategic plan

Background

GO Freight is a legal entity incorporated under the laws of .... in ......, 2007. The company has been registered with the Ministry of Transport as a third party freight services company. Appropriate insurance will be put in place for liabilities and other commercial risks. The company is presently owned 50/50 by .... and .... who will also share management, sales and operations responsibilities.

The strategic objectives and action plan for the business are summarized below.

Strategic Objectives:

9. Open the business and confirm the first major customer commitments by ..... , 20__.

10. Complete the first full year of operation with:

- Sales exceeding $3,000,000
- Profitability demonstrated by before tax income of at least $200,000
- Cash flow positive and net debt at zero.

11. Be recognized as an industry leader in third party logistics for truck freight by major shippers in our target markets within three years.
12. Achieve continued, stable, profitable growth to sales exceeding $5,000,000 per year within five years.

Action Plan:

7. Complete a documented Business Plan including financial projections to confirm initial bank financing by ..... , 20___.
8. Acquire premises by November 15th and install equipment and services to open for business on December 1st, 20___.
9. Introduce GO Freight to key customer contacts and develop opportunities to commence shipping services in early December.
10. Engage a third employee to assist with administration and customer service at GO Freight to start on December 15th, 20___.
11. Prepare a marketing brochure and web site to promote our services by January 31st, 20___.
12. Achieve the $200,000 in monthly revenue by March 31, 20___.
13. Provide contracted services for at least five major shippers by June 30th, 20___ and add at least one new customer per month until the end of 20___.

These strategic objectives and the action plan with stated goals and milestones will be the planning guide for management through the first year of operations.

19. Management team

A primary competitive strength of GO Freight arises from the combined knowledge, skills and experience of its management team. The key members who are dedicated to achieving the company's objectives are:

- Name, title, role, responsibilities
    - o   Summary background ....
- Name, title, role, responsibilities
    - o   Summary background ....

Additional information on each of these individuals is provided in more detail in Appendix ... along with an initial organizational structure. Additional experienced resources will be engaged as required. A candidate for the third position as Office Manager has already been identified.

The expected staffing costs are included with the financial schedules of Appendix A.

20. Service offering

GO Freight will offer traffic management solutions for full truckloads, including domestic, import/export, refrigerated trucks, and flat-bed trucks.

GO Freight will focus on delivering services that are cost effective with dependable performance and high levels of customer service.

GO Freight will provide transportation management services including the following:

- Audit and analysis of traffic patterns to determine specific handling requirements.
- Developing least-cost solutions to meet the shipper's needs.
- Contracting with the appropriate carriers to meet the desired service levels for our customers.

GO Freight will also provide backhaul opportunities from other carriers who do not have representation in our area. These carriers are already delivering into the region and have space available for low cost back-hauls that GO Freight can fill effectively and increase their revenues while also delivering cost savings to the shippers.

21. Marketing and sales plan

The company has limited plans for marketing activities. The corporate identity and marketing messages will be communicated through a simple marketing brochure and a well-designed basic website. These are already in process so that they will be available to support early sales activities. No direct advertising or publicity campaigns are currently planned other than some listings in trade industry directories both online and in trade publications.

The company principals will maintain their active participation in local traffic clubs, industry associations and transportation conferences and trade shows in order to keep in touch with their contact network and promote GO Freight.

Business development and sales growth will be achieved by continuous direct sales efforts and soliciting leads and referrals from our current customer contacts.

22. Operations plan

Location and Facilities

GO Freight will be centrally located commercial offices of the industrial park at ...., _____ .

Operating Processes

The services of GO Freight are focused on full truckload freight management for large shippers in our region. Operating processes will be dedicated to providing outstanding levels of customer service by selecting the most appropriate carriers, monitoring performance levels and maintaining constant communication with our customers.

Office systems, information technology and telecommunications will all support those service objectives. Additional staff will be selected, recruited, trained and compensated so that they are also supportive of high levels of performance and customer service.

23. Risk analysis

The business risks are understood by management and will be managed to the minimum possible. These risks arise from potential changes in market or economic conditions that are not controllable by GO Freight and from business conditions that are internal to GO Freight and can be minimized.

Market risks:

1. Economic conditions.

    Changes in government regulations, taxes, fees, foreign exchange, interest rates or security requirements will affect all players at the same time and should not provide any competitive advantage/disadvantage.

2. General decline in target markets.

   This risk is limited by the strategy of diversification in various markets and lack of dependence on any single large customer (except for _____ in the first year).

3. New business models, foreign competitors.

   Overland freight is a very hands-on, regional business that cannot be displaced by offshore sources or an online business model.

4. Changes in technology.

   New tools in IT or telecommunications may affect costs, processes, and client expectations but GO Freight is already using the latest technologies available and will keep on top of new tools that may become available.

Business risks:

1. Availability of key personnel

   Partners will sign a shareholders agreement for their mutual protection and acquire key-man life insurance on each other. GO Freight will manage employees to ensure high motivation and retention, but will also take the precautions of having signed confidentiality, non-conflict of interest and non-competition agreements where they are appropriate.

2. Loss of major suppliers

   Protection from interruption of service will be achieved by maintaining alternative freight carriers and other service providers.

3. Systems and facilities risks

   GO Freight will take reasonable precautions to protect systems and facilities and also maintain commercial insurance against business interruption.

3. Regulatory

GO Freight will maintain all regulatory approvals as necessary.

The financial projections show that GO Freight's business model has strong revenue potential that delivers a high return on investment and is attractive in spite of these known business risks.

24. Financial plan

Initial financial analysis shows that full operating costs can be recovered at a break-even sales level of $ 1.8 million in freight revenue per year. The first year is expected to be almost double that figure.

A detailed financial plan is attached. The Financial Plan includes the following:

- Opening Balance Sheet and Financial Requirements
- Sales Revenue and Gross Profit Projections
- Organisation Plan
- Expense Forecast
- Net Income and ROI Projections
- Cash Flow Forecast
- Investment Forecast
- Projected Balance Sheets

This Business Plan has been prepared to describe the business opportunity, the strategy, the operating plan, and the expected financial results.

Thank you for your interest in reviewing our Business Plan.

APPENDICES:

A. Financial plan
B. Management team
C. Marketing brochure
D. Market research data
E. Service cost estimates, comparative quotes
F. Letters of reference, testimonials
H. Other relevant documents…

Sample Financial Projections – Happy Pets Center Inc.

The required financial projections are shown in the following pages for a typical company (Happy Pets Inc.) with a mix of product and service revenues.

They include:

- Initial Balance Sheet showing the start-up costs and planned sources of financing
- Sales, Revenue and Gross Margin forecasts
- Variable and fixed expenses, Profit and Loss Projections and an estimate of equity value
- Cash Flow Projections
- Balance Sheet Projections
- Notes on the assumptions used and the basis for all the estimated values

These examples will give you some ideas on how to present your own financials and you can then develop spreadsheets to evaluate various scenarios and assumptions, until you are satisfied with the planned results.

Be sure to check your final draft so that the business plan text is consistent with the financial results that you show in your Appendix.

Happy Pets Center – Financial Projections

Expansion Start-up Requirements:

	Opening Balance Sheet	Required for Start-up*	Total:
Assets:			
Cash	5,000	0	5,000
Inventory	0	65,000	65,000
Accounts Receivable	0		0
Advances Receivable	0		0
Capital Equipment (net)	0		0
Leasehold improvements*	0	69,850	69,850
Incorporation	1,500	0	1,500
Capital Equipment Sub-total:	1,500	69,850	71,350
Pre-paid Expenses:			
Financing costs	1,500	985	2,485
Professional fees	7,500	10,000	17,500
Start-up expense & deposits	5,000	7,000	12,000
Expense Sub-total:	14,000	17,985	31,985
Total Funding Requirements:	20,500	152,835	173,335
Sources of financing:			
Current liabilities	0		0
Current bank loans	10,500	0	10,500
Shareholder loans	0	0	0
New lending		120,000	120,000
Retained Earnings	0		0
Shareholder Capital	10,000	0	10,000
New Equity Investment		32,835	32,835
Total Equity	10,000	32,835	42,835
Total Financing:	20,500	152,835	173,335

* Details of expansion start-up costs attached.

Capital expenditures:	Start-up Costs	Year 2 TOTAL:	Year 3 TOTAL:
Retail Store area: (4000 sq. ft.)			
Shelving	$ 7,250.00		
Interior décor	$ 1,200.00		
Cash register with scanner	$ 2,250.00		
Inventory Control software	$ 5,000.00		$ 500.00
Office computers & equip.	$ 2,500.00	$ 1,500.00	
Sub-total:	**$ 18,200.00**	**$ 1,500.00**	**$ 500.00**
Reception area (480 sq.ft.)	$ 5,000.00		
Washrooms (2) (100 sq.ft.)	$ 2,000.00		
Veterinary office & equip. (150 sq.ft.)	$ 7,000.00		
Sub-total:	**$ 14,000.00**	**$ -**	**$ -**
Hydraulic tables (2)	$ 4,000.00		
Kennels (2)	$ 4,000.00		
Other equipment, furnishings	$ 950.00	$ 1,500.00	$ 1,500.00
Sub-total:	**$ 8,950.00**	**$ 1,500.00**	**$ 1,500.00**
Class Room Furniture & Equipment (seating 20)	$ 3,700.00		$ 1,500.00
Signage	$ 5,000.00		
Furnishing & fixtures	$ 12,500.00	$ 1,500.00	$ 1,500.00
Interior decoration	$ 7,500.00		
Sub-total:	**$ 25,000.00**	**$ 1,500.00**	**$ 1,500.00**
Total Capital Expenditures	**$ 69,850.00**	**$ 4,500.00**	**$ 5,000.00**

Sales Revenue & Gross Margin Forecast: Schedule 1.

Pet Centre:	Monthly sales	Start-up 3-mos	Year 1 TOTAL:	Year 2 TOTAL:	Year 3 TOTAL:
Sales - nutrition	*Monthly*	2	Growth @	30%	15%
Revenue	$ 50,000	100.0	550.0	715.0	822.3
Sales - pet accessories	*Monthly*	2			
Revenue @ 30% of food	$ 15,000	30.0	165.0	214.5	246.7
Grooming services	*hours*	300			
Fees @ $50/hour	$ 50	15.0	87.0	113.1	130.1
Veterinary Services	*hours*	320			
Fees @ $115/hr	$ 115	36.8	202.4	263.1	302.6
Veterinary Care Produc	*Monthly*				
Revenue @ 50% of fees	50%	18.4	101.2	131.6	151.3
Nutritional Supplement	*Monthly*	2			
Revenue	$ 17,500	35.0	192.5	250.3	287.8
Other: therapy, classes, etc.		2			
Revenue @ $250/class	$ 250	0.5	2.8	3.6	4.1
TOTAL REVENUE:		**235.7**	**1300.9**	**1691.1**	**1944.8**
Product & Service Costs	**% of sales**				
Nutrition products	65%	65.0	357.5	464.8	534.5
Accessories	55%	16.5	90.8	118.0	135.7
Groomers cost	50%	7.5	43.5	56.6	65.0
Veterinarian	75%	27.6	151.8	197.3	226.9
Vet. Product costs	60%	11.0	60.7	78.9	90.8
Nutritional Supplements	65%	22.8	125.1	162.7	187.1
Transport & stocking	0.5%	0.9	5.0	6.6	7.5
Sales commissions	0.0%	0.0	0.0	0.0	0.0
Total Cost of Sales:		**151.3**	**834.4**	**1084.8**	**1247.5**
GROSS MARGIN $:		**84.4**	**466.4**	**606.3**	**697.3**
Gross Margin %:		35.8%	35.9%	35.9%	35.9%

Organization Plan:		Schedule 2.		
		Year 1 TOTAL:	Year 2 TOTAL:	Year 3 TOTAL:
NO. OF PLANNED STAFF:				
General Manager		1	1	1
Store Manager		1	1	1
Retail Sales staff*		4	4	6
Finance & Admin.		1	1	1
Clinic receptionist		1	1	1
Veterinary technician		1	1.5	1.5
TOTAL STAFF :		9	9.5	11.5
EXPENSE/EMPLOYEE:	**nnual Salary**			
General Manager	$ 40,000	3.8	3.8	3.8
Store Manager	$ 35,000	3.4	3.4	3.4
Retail Sales staff*	$ 20,800	2.0	2.0	2.0
Finance & Admin.	$ 35,000	3.4	3.4	3.4
Clinic receptionist	$ 24,000	2.3	2.3	2.3
Veterinary technician	$ 30,000	2.9	2.9	2.9
TOTAL STAFF EXPENSE: ($1000's)				
General Manager		46.0	46.0	46.0
Store Manager		40.3	40.3	40.3
Retail Sales staff*		95.7	95.7	143.5
Finance & Admin.		40.3	40.3	40.3
Clinic receptionist		27.6	27.6	27.6
Veterinary technician		34.5	51.8	51.8
TOTAL:		284.3	301.5	349.4

* Note: Retail sales staff @ average $10.00/hour.

Expense Forecast:		Start-up 3-mos	Schedule 3. Year 1 TOTAL:	Year 2 TOTAL:	Year 3 TOTAL:
OPERATING EXPENSE:					
*Total Staff:		9	9	9.5	11.5
*Total Staff Costs:		**71.1**	**284.3**	**301.5**	**349.4**
% of Staff Costs:					
Admin. & Office Expense	5.0%	3.6	14.2	15.1	17.5
Pre-paid Start-up Expenses		31.99	32.0		
Rent		24.75	99.0	102.0	105.0
Rent from Vet. Clinic & Grooming		Included	0.0	0.0	0.0
Business Insurance & Taxes		3.0	12.0	12.0	15.0
Telecom/Internet, Utilities		2.3	9.0	9.0	12.0
Professional Fees		3.0	9.5	9.5	12.5
Total O/H & Admin.		**68.5**	**175.7**	**147.5**	**162.0**
Sales & Marketing:					
Marketing materials		2.5	4.0	7.5	7.5
Advertising & Promotion		7.5	21.0	25.0	30.0
Web Site Maintenance			6.5	2.5	2.5
Total Sales & Mktg. Exp.:		**10.0**	**31.5**	**35.0**	**40.0**
Total Operating Expense:		**149.6**	**491.5**	**484.1**	**551.4**
* See Schedule 2 for details: Organization Plan					

Summary - Net Income: Schedule 4.

		Monthly			Year 1	Year 2	Year 3
		M4	M5	M6	TOTAL:	TOTAL:	TOTAL:
TOTAL REVENUE:		118.4	118.4	118.4	1300.9	1691.1	1944.8
Total Cost of Sales:		75.9	75.9	75.9	834.4	1084.77	1247.486
GROSS MARGIN $:		**42.4**	**42.4**	**42.4**	**466.4**	**606.3**	**697.3**
Gross Margin %:		35.9%	35.9%	35.9%	35.9%	35.9%	35.9%
OPERATING EXPENSE:							
*Total Staff Costs:		23.7	23.7	23.7	284.3	301.5	349.4
Total O/H & Admin.		12.2	12.2	12.2	175.7	147.5	162.0
Sales & Mktg Expense		1.5	1.5	1.5	31.5	35.0	40.0
Bank charges & Interest	6.0%	0.7	0.7	0.7	9.8	-1.2	-4.2
Depreciation		0.0	0.0	0.0	14.3	15.2	16.2
Total Expense:		**38.0**	**38.0**	**38.0**	**515.5**	**498.1**	**563.4**
NET INCOME Before Tax:		**4.4**	**4.4**	**4.4**	**-49.1**	**108.3**	**133.9**
Net Income %:		4%	3.7%	3.7%	-3.8%	6.4%	6.9%
Less income taxes	18.0%				-8.8	19.5	24.1
Net Income after tax:					-40.3	88.8	109.8
Return on Total Assets					**-19.9%**	**25.6%**	**21.5%**
Return on Equity:					**-94.0%**	**207.2%**	**256.4%**
Net Present Value of 5-years Net Inc	discounted @				**-33.6**	**61.6**	**63.5**
			BUSINESS VALUE:		$	91,627	

Cash Flow Forecast: Summary   ($1,0(Schedule 5.

	Opening Balances	Monthly M4	M5	M6	Year 1 TOTAL:	Year 2 TOTAL:	Year 3 TOTAL:
MONTHLY RECEIPTS:							
Initial cash balance	**5.0**				0.0		
Additional sources					0.0		
Cash received from sales		118.4	118.4	118.4	1300.9	1691.1	1944.8
TOTAL CASH INFLOW:		**118.4**	**118.4**	**118.4**	**1300.9**	**1691.1**	**1944.8**
CASH PAYMENTS:							
Total Cost of Sales		75.9	75.9	75.9	834.4	1084.8	1247.5
Monthly Operating Exp.		37.4	37.4	37.4	491.5	484.1	551.4
Capital & Start-up Costs		0.0	0.0	0.0	173.3	4.5	5.0
Income Taxes					-8.8	19.5	24.1
Dividends paid					0.0	0.0	0.0
TOTAL CASH OUTFLOW:		**113.3**	**113.3**	**113.3**	**1490.4**	**1592.8**	**1828.0**
CASH SURPLUS/SHORT:		**5.1**	**5.1**	**5.1**	**-189.6**	**98.3**	**116.8**
ADDITIONAL CASH IN:							
Shareholders' Equity	10.0				10.0	0.0	0.0
Additional Equity	32.8				32.8	0.0	0.0
CUM. EQUITY:	**42.8**	42.8	42.8	42.8	42.8	42.8	42.8
Bank Loans	10.5				10.5	0.0	0.0
Shareholder loans	0.0				0.0	0.0	0.0
Additional financing	120.0	0.0			0.0	-150.0	-50.0
CUM. DEBT:	**130.5**	130.5	130.5	130.5	130.5	-19.5	-69.5
NET CASH FLOW(+/-)		**5.1**	**5.1**	**5.1**	**-136.2**	**98.3**	**116.8**
CUM. CASH BALANCE(+/-):	**5.0**	**-55.1**	**-50.1**	**-45.0**	**-11.2**	**87.0**	**203.9**

Projected Balance Sheet	$1000's Opening Balance Sheet	Year 1	Year 2	Year 3
Assets:				
Cash	5.0	-11.2	87.0	203.9
Inventory	65.0	216.8	281.9	324.1
Accounts Receivable	0.0	0.0	0.0	0.0
Advances Receivable	0.0	0.0	0.0	0.0
Capital Equipment	71.4	71.4	75.9	80.9
Less Depreciation @ avg. 20%	0.0	14.3	15.2	16.2
Net Capital Assets:	71.4	57.1	60.7	64.7
Total Assets:	141.4	262.7	429.6	592.7
Liabilities:				
Short-term liabilities	-32.0	129.6	357.8	461.0
Bank loans	130.5	130.5	-19.5	-69.5
Shareholders Loans	0.0			
Shareholders' Equity	42.8	42.8	42.8	42.8
Cum. Retained Earnings	0.0	-40.3	48.5	158.3
Total Liabilities:	141.4	262.7	429.6	592.7

MORE RESOURCES FROM UNCLE RALPH

As a complement to this Guide and for additional ideas, information and inspiration to build and grow your business, you may be interested in these resources from Uncle Ralph:

DIYBusinessPlan.com
http://www.diybusinessplan.com/

Learn about Entrepreneurship
http://learningentrepreneurship.com

Ezine Articles on Business and Entrepreneurship
http://ezinearticles.com/?expert=Delvin R. Chatterson

Uncle Ralphs' e2eForum Blog
http://e2eforum1.blogspot.ca

Business is Like Golf Blog:
http://businessislikegolf.blogspot.com/

Or follow Del on:

LinkedIn: http://ca.linkedin.com/in/delchatterson

Twitter: http://twitter.com/Del UncleRalph

Facebook: https://www.facebook.com/YourUncleRalph

And don't miss Uncle Ralph's new book for Entrepreneurs:

"Don't Do It the Hard Way"

"A wise man learns from the mistakes of others;
only a fool insists on making his own".
©2014

ADDITIONAL RESOURCES
USED AND RECOMMENDED

In the course of preparing Business Plans for myself or clients and while preparing to write this Do-It-Yourself Guide, I have used many external resources, which I also recommend to the reader for additional insights and information to help you prepare a successful business plan that gets the results that you want.

You will also find input to consider against my own approach and advice that may be more relevant to your specific needs.

Guides and Textbooks:

Check at your local business school, university or college library and you will find certainly find useful references on business management issues, entrepreneurship and business planning.

At Concordia University I used these two textbooks to complement my own material for the courses in Financial Management and Business Planning.:

> *Business Plan, Business Reality*, James R. Skinner, Second Edition
>
> *Principles of Corporate Finance*, Gitman & Hennessy, Second Canadian Edition

Additional business planning guides may be available from your accountant or bank and check what your friends and colleagues recommend. After you recommend "*The Complete Do-It-Yourself Guide to Business Plans*", of course.

Online Resources

Most banks, business consulting firms and other professionals offering services to entrepreneurs provide online access to brochures, guidelines, checklists and even templates. You will also find many vendors of software tools that can be purchased and downloaded to "automatically" prepare a business plan from your input – these I do not recommend. They are usually a poor fit to your specific plan and very difficult to adapt to your circumstances. Output looks computer-generated from a "fill-in-the-blanks" form and will not be well received.

About the Author

Del Chatterson is an experienced consultant, entrepreneur and executive. His company, **DirectTech Solutions**, provides strategic advisory services to business owners, managers and entrepreneurs.

His focus is: *"Creative, Practical Business Solutions. Delivered."*

Del is dedicated to helping entrepreneurs to be better and to do better.

He has helped businesses at all stages: from start-up through to the operating and management challenges of achieving sustainable growth and profitability and the exit strategies for management transition and succession plans.

His expertise is most often applied in assessing business performance and developing strategic plans to achieve higher levels of performance and profitability.

Del has lectured at Concordia and McGill Universities on entrepreneurship, financial management and business planning. He has given seminars and workshops on business management and entrepreneurship issues and continues to offer ideas, information and inspiration for entrepreneurs through his Blogs, articles and books under the persona of "Uncle Ralph".

Del is an MBA and Engineer with a wealth of business management and consulting experience. He has been successful in both corporate and entrepreneurial environments with particular expertise in distribution, professional services and technology businesses.

Del is a valuable resource to business managers and entrepreneurs for strategic insights based on his perceptive market assessments and his rigorous financial analysis.

Your Uncle Ralph

Delvin R. Chatterson

CPSIA information can be obtained at www.ICGtesting.com
Printed in the USA
BVOW01s1111200414

351172BV00001B/21/P